MW01004781

# ITALIAN

*Food*
*&*
*Life*

## R U L E S

## ALSO BY ANN REAVIS

Italian Food Rules

Italian Life Rules

Murder at Mountain Vista

The Case of the Pilfered Pills

Death at the Duomo

Cats of Italy

# ITALIAN
## *Food*
## *& Life*
### RULES

BY
ANN REAVIS

**ITALIAN FOOD & LIFE RULES**

Copyright © 2016 Ann J. Reavis
All rights reserved.

ISBN-13: 978-1540395757
ISBN-10: 1540395758


Published by Caldera Books
Email: calderabooks@gmail.com

Cover by Kelly Crimi
Interior book design by Bob Houston eBook Formatting

Without limiting the rights under copyright reserved above, no part of this publication may be reproduced, stored in, or introduced into a retrieval system, or transmitted, in any form, or by any means (electronic, mechanical, photocopying, recording, or otherwise) without the prior written permission of the copyright holder of the book.

First Edition (December 1, 2016)

*For Francesca*

# CONTENTS

# ITALIAN

## *Food*

## R U L E S

# FOREWORD

It is a joy to learn something new and surprising. As a teacher, it is even better when I learn from a student.

Ann Reavis, a San Francisco lawyer in search of any enlightenment that nine months in Italy could bring her, walked into my Italian grammar class in Massa Marittima, near the Tuscan coast, in 1998. To be kind, let's say that she had no ear for my melodic language.

Changing focus, she sought to learn to expand her kitchen skills beyond admittedly delicious chocolate chip cookies and carrot cake to include Florentine and Tuscan recipes. I was conducting cooking classes for Americans and other tourists. Ann, unfortunately, could never master a passable *soffritto* or achieve *al dente* when it came to cooking pasta.

I was ready to give up on the notion that Ann was ever going to awaken to the state of being Italian even for a day, but then we started to delve into the customs and practices that make Italian food authentic. Maybe it is the lawyer's need for defined rules and precedents, or Ann's love for research that, combined with her passion for eating, if not cooking, Italian food led her to collect what she came to call "Italian Food Rules."

After nine months in Florence became over fifteen years in Italy, Ann is still clearly American, but she knows more than most Italians about the basis of the food practices that are passed down from generation to generation. Her delight in each discovery has frequently been shared in her writing on TuscanTraveler.com and, now, in this enchanting book.

The facts, fictions, history and reasons behind the Italian Food Rules, as well as the revelation of the mere existence of so many customs or edicts, will assist any visitor to Italy by making their stay easier, less confusing, and richer. For Italians, their response to reading Ann's list of the rules is usually *"giusto, giusto"* ("exactly right") and then delight when they read the rationale and history of the gastronomic commandments passed down from their grandmothers.

I never knew where Caesar Salad originated (certainly not Italy), or why spaghetti with meatballs was considered an Italian dish, or why Americans always wanted a bowl of olive oil with a squiggle of balsamic vinegar delivered immediately to the table when dining at a trattoria. I enjoy eating *lampredotto* and *lardo* on a regular basis, being very familiar with these Tuscan specialties, but I never thought much about their origins in Italian history until Ann started asking questions, urging me to translate at Florentine tripe stands, and traveling to Colonnata to see where herbed lard is aged.

The bricks that form the foundation of the most loved cuisine in the world today are important and should be preserved. Ann Reavis has given us the gift of memory in her light and amusing book of Italian Food Rules.

Francesca Maria Boni, Florence

# BY WAY OF INTRODUCTION

In Italy they love making rules, and they obey very few…except when it comes to food. The Italian Food Rules may as well be carved in marble. They will not change and you violate them at your peril.

I grew up during the '50s in the American West where there were no food rules. TV dinners vied with Chef Boyardee canned spaghetti and meatballs. Sweet potatoes were topped with marshmallows. A fried egg smothered in ketchup or a breakfast burrito was equally good in the morning. Iced tea paired well with any food. A Filet O'Fish, French fries, and a Big Gulp were road food–better tasting eaten in the car, than out.

Then I moved to San Francisco and my junk food days were over. Now I was dining on all of the fine cuisines of the world, including at some of the best Italian restaurants in America. (Full disclosure: I still scarfed down the occasional pint of ice cream for dinner.)

I thought I knew Italian cuisine when I arrived in Italy in 1998 for what turned out to be a fifteen-year sojourn. I may have been able to recognize Italian food, but I had no clue about the Italian Food Rules. I broke every single one of them.

The Italian Food Rules have a long history. Some traveled with Catherine de' Medici to France in the 16th century. Others are even older.

Despite the attempts by outsiders to influence the politics and cultural life of the Italian peninsula for the past millennium, the Italian people have remained largely homogenous. They will argue there are insurmountable regional differences in their recipes, but outsiders will be hard pressed to understand what all the fuss is about. Since Italians do not generally move far from home, the food traditions are passed on unchanged from generation to generation. Italian Food Rules practiced 200 years ago are still valid today.

The Italian food culture encourages eating foods that are in season and grown locally, which could be considered two of the most important Italian Food Rules. It is little wonder that the Slow Food movement started in Italy.

Founded in 1989 in the Piemonte region to counter the rise in Italy of fast food, the organization's interests grew to include the disappearance of local food culture and traditional ingredients. Slow Food is now a grassroots organization with over 100,000 supporters in 150 countries around the world, who are linking the pleasure of good food with a commitment to their community and the environment. The organization's philosophy has its basis in the Italian Food Rules.

This small book just skims the surface of the Italian Food Rules. Although some Italians might rightly argue that one or two of these Rules don't apply to their region or their small town, this book is meant to be of some assistance to the visitor who wants to try to be Italian at least once in a lifetime.

# DON'T DRINK CAPPUCCINO
# AFTER TEN IN THE MORNING

To order a cappuccino after lunch is a direct and major violation of an Italian Food Rule. Italians believe the fresh whole milk that makes up over half of the contents of cappuccino plays havoc with digestion. To order a cappuccino after 10am, unless you are breakfasting after said hour, is seen as suspect behavior worthy of at least a slight frown, advancing to a worried shake of the head, and can escalate to outright ridicule.

To the Italians, milk is almost a meal in itself. So having a cappuccino at the neighborhood bar in the morning on the way to work or school requires no other food to be considered a complete breakfast. (A small pastry may be included, but not always.) Cappuccino is more milk than coffee, so it is full of calories. Perhaps the reasoning is that slender Italians (the ones who don't order the pastry) are more likely to burn off the calories through the day. Drunk later, those pesky calories stay on the hips.

Some say that cappuccino is best in the morning

because the milk has lactose (a sugar) and the body absorbs the lactose and milk fat quickly, so the carbohydrate energy is available immediately before the caffeine stimulant kicks in.

The real reason behind the Food Rule, however, is that Italians are firmly convinced that drinking milk after any meal will mess up the stomach's ability to digest food properly. So having a cappuccino at any time after lunch, or after dinner, in Italy is unthinkable.

Tourists, therefore, shouldn't be shocked when the waiter refuses to grant their cappuccino requests "for your own health."

## DID YOU KNOW?

• No slice of lemon or lemon peel with espresso.
• If you must have milk in your after-meal coffee, order *caffè macchiato* (stained coffee).
• Coffee can be served with a shot of alcohol (grappa, cognac, rum), order *caffè corretto*.
• There are no frappuccinos in Italy, order *caffè shakerato*.
• *Caffè* is to be drunk standing at a bar or at the table after a meal.
• Italians do not order double espresso—espresso is a short drink.

# DON'T ASK FOR HALF & HALF OR SOY MILK FOR YOUR COFFEE

Is it a sign of the end of culture when the choices, or individual demands, get too numerous? The babel of maladies, desires, and requests bombard us–"I'm lactose intolerant. Do you have lactose-free milk or soy?" "I want just the essence of coffee, can you add more cream, or, better yet, whipped cream?" "I'm on a diet–skim milk, please." "I want whole milk–cold." "I want Half & Half–do you know what that is–like, half cream, half milk? It sometimes comes in a tiny plastic container, back home?"

Coffee is simple in Italy. You can find it the following ways in any coffee bar:

*un caffè*–this is a single-shot espresso, but don't call it espresso, no Italian does. Do not order *un caffè doppio*–a double espresso or wait a couple of hours, as the Italians do, for your next dose.

*cappuccino* and *caffellatte*–before 10am.

*caffè macchiato* or *latte macchiato*–an espresso with a dash of milk or a hot milk with a dash of coffee (remember, mornings only).

*caffè corretto*–the Italian male's (gender specific and usually of the blue–collar variety) early morning pick-me-up, an espresso "corrected" with a shot of brandy or grappa.

*caffè freddo* or *cappuccino freddo*–iced espresso or cappuccino, possibly with sugar added by the barista.

*un caffè lungo* or *un caffè ristretto*–more or less water in an *espresso*) or ask for an *americano* if you want the traditional cup o' joe.

There are a couple of regional exceptions. In Naples, the locals order un *caffè alla nocciola*–a frothy espresso with hazelnut cream. In Milan, the fashionistas ask for *un marocchino*, an upside-down *cappuccino*, served in a small glass that is first sprinkled with cocoa powder, then hit with a bit of frothed milk, then finished off with a shot of espresso.

# DON'T ASK FOR COFFEE "TO GO"

It is a simple joy for many Americans to begin their multi-tasking day with a long coffee "to go." They prepare the brew in their own special way and pour it into a hi-tech stainless steel sippy cup that fits perfectly in the cup holder of their SUV. Or they stop a block from the office, pull out their Starbucks Reward Card and continue down the street scalding their palate with that first impatient sip.

Think of the overwhelming joy of American commuters when Starbucks and Dunkin' Donuts put in drive-through windows.

Italians don't believe in delayed gratification. Their morning *cappuccino* or afternoon *espresso* must be made with perfectly ground, roasted Arabica coffee beans from the doser grinder, tamped into the filter basket of a properly pre-heated Italian-made coffee machine by a *barista* who has been doing the same repetitive action for 20 years. Italians will immediately drink the *espresso* (three sips) or *cappuccino* (ten sips) from the appropriate sized ceramic cup while standing at the bar where their fathers and grandfathers stood before them.

Some Italians have never sipped a coffee outside of a coffee bar—not at home, or a friend's home, and certainly not out of a paper cup. The only exception for these hard-liners is a very occasional *espresso* at the end of a meal in a restaurant.

The basis of the Food Rule is quality—of the coffee bean, the coffee machine, the cup and the *barista*. This assures the consistent temperature, the appropriate strength, the correct amount (never a double *espresso*), and the right amount and temperature of any added milk (a few drips for a *macchiato* and never "extra cream" for a *cappuccino*).

The experience is immediate and satisfying. If one part of the process goes awry the whole day could be ruined.

# ITALIANS ONLY DRINK TEA
# WHEN THEY ARE SICK

Tea drinkers of the U.K. and the U.S. might as well give up the idea of a good "cuppa" in Italy. Italians only drink tea when they are sick–at home.

You can ask for, and receive, hot tea in a coffee bar. First, the *barista* will give you a searching glance from a distance to see if you are obviously infectious. Then, he will run some hot water out of the coffee machine into a *cappuccino* cup. The water will be un-filtered tap water, which may taste great, but in Flor-ence, for example, is highly mineralized, a taste hidden easily by coffee, but not by tea. And, having passed through the coffee machine, the water will have the odor, if not the taste, of stale coffee.

The water may or may not be of sufficient temperature to brew tea from the generic tea bag (or, perhaps, Lipton or Twinings in an upscale bar). The tea bag will be wrapped in its paper cover, resting in the saucer of the rapidly cooling cup of water.

If you go out to dinner at the home of an Italian friend, carry your own tea bags. Their cupboards will only contain chamomile tea bags or *tisane della salute*. Also, be prepared for the sympathetic look and an inquiry about how long you have been feeling "under the weather." Finally, your friends may not have cups for tea, only tiny cups for espresso. A water glass can substitute for a teacup, but don't fill it too full, only the top edge will stay cool enough to touch.

As for your own vacation rental in Italy: plan to bring an electric kettle, a Brita pitcher with filters, and your favorite tea. In cities, specialty grocery stores will carry good tea, but at high prices.

Get used to the question *"Prendiamo un caffè?"* and the look you will get when you say you drink tea. As a foreigner, you will be given a pass. Imagine a tea-loving, coffee-hating Italian–his life would be like being a vegetarian at a Texas barbecue...every single day of the year.

# DON'T DIP BREAD IN OLIVE OIL

It was over twenty years ago when I first broke the Italian Food Rule: Don't Dip Bread in Olive Oil. Or, to clarify: Don't serve bread with a bowl of olive oil with a swirl of balsamic vinegar as an appetizer (or any other part of the meal).

Back to my first experience: I was trying a new restaurant in San Francisco. I watched with curiosity as our waiter presented with a flourish a thin sliced baguette of warm sourdough bread and a bowl of deep green extra virgin olive oil. But he didn't stop there. With some sleight of hand, he then produced a small bottle of balsamic vinegar and created a floating purplish *S* on the surface of the oil.

Noting our bemused expressions, he explained that the proper procedure was to dip a bite of torn bread into the oil, catching a smidgen of the *aceto balsamico* (I can't remember if he actually said "*aceto balsamico*") and pop it into one's mouth. I caught on immediately and, for the next five years or so, I savored bread dipped in olive oil throughout the fine restaurants of San Francisco and across the United

States.

In 1998, I arrived in Italy and it was immediately apparent that there was absolutely no practice of setting bowls of olive oil on the table so customers could munch on bread before the *antipasti* arrived. In fact, then and now, there may not be bread on the table until the main course is served (see Don't Eat Bread with Pasta).

However, by the turn of the millennium, most Americans, including those from places like Iowa and Texas, were hooked on olive oil and bread. They arrived in droves on Italian shores expecting to be served olive oil, bread, and even, that squiggle of balsamic vinegar, in the trattorias and fine restaurants across Italy.

In the beginning, Italian waiters (and restaurant owners) were simply confused—why all of this demand for olive oil when there was no food on which to put it? But then they swiftly moved from being perplexed to being appalled.

Why appalled, you ask? Certainly Americans (and tourists of all nationalities) had broken Italian Food Rules before, but those infractions paled in comparison with what happened when Americans, olive oil, and bread were combined. It was a catastrophe: A tourist asks for bread. The waiter complies, sneering a bit because he knows that eating bread before a meal ruins the appetite and leads to fat. Then the tourist throws the waiter an impatient look and asks for the olive oil.

Now the waiter quits sneering. He either says

that there is no olive oil for the dining room (salads are dressed in the kitchen; pasta and veggies get their last splash from the chef; same with the main courses). Or, he brings a large bottle of olive oil– from the kitchen or the waiters' service stand–to the table.

You say you don't understand the problem? Imagine the table in our hypothetical trattoria. Now there is a basket of bread and a bottle of olive oil in the center by the small candle or tiny floral centerpiece. There are four paper placemats, each topped with a knife and fork and a napkin. What do the Americans do? They have stretched to ask for *pane* and *olio*, using the right words. They have no further language resources or patience for *piatto* (plate), and *ciotolina* or *piccola ciotola* (little bowl), or any other tableware word, and frankly they are a bit miffed that the olive oil didn't come served in a bowl.

So they take a slice of bread, place it on their paper placemat, and gingerly aim the spout of the large olive oil bottle at the center, trying desperately not to run over the crusty edges. Of course, the olive oil, poured by even the most careful person, soaks through the light Italian bread, onto the placemat or napkin underneath.

The tourist is upset and embarrassed, and the waiter is appalled and apoplectic. Now, add a cotton tablecloth under our hypothetical placemats and you see how the problem escalates. I do not exaggerate here for effect. I have seen both situations with my own eyes.

There are a few good reasons for the Italian Food Rule: Don't Dip Bread in Olive Oil. Fine Italian extra virgin olive oil the only type to eat with bread— is expensive. To place a bowl of olive oil on the table in front of Italians guarantees the waste of excess oil because Italians don't eat bread before they start their meal. (Some might argue that Americans will wipe the bowl clean, but remember Italian Food Rules were not created with Americans in mind.) Italians, also, aren't given to eating out of a communal bowl (dipping a hunk of bread in olive oil, taking a bite and then dipping it back in the same oil would cause an Italian to go pale with visions of bacteria). There is, also, the possibility of drips. Italians avoid potential messes. This list probably just skims the surface of the reasons behind the Rule.

As for that *S* of *aceto balsamico* floating on the oil…there is probably an extra penalty for adding that to the crime. Italians do not put balsamic vinegar on bread. Italians do not make a salad dressing with balsamic vinegar and olive oil (red wine vinegar only). Traditional *aceto balsamico* is wildly expensive, exquisitely good and should never be wasted or drowned in olive oil.

But if oil and bread are so good together, why don't the Italians give in? Well, Italians do eat bread with extra virgin olive oil on top. The dish is called *fettunta* from *fetta* (slice) and *unta* (oily)–an "oily slice". The bread is not dipped in oil. A slice of bread is toasted (preferably over a flame), rubbed while still warm with a halved clove of fresh garlic, and placed on a plate. Fresh extra virgin olive oil is poured over the slice of bread and salt is added to taste. It is difficult to find this dish in a restaurant because it is considered simple home food, not worthy of a dining experience and difficult to price since it is basically a slice of bread with a splash of olive oil.

When in Italy, save the dipping of bread in olive oil for a formal tasting of the year's new oil in December and January where the purpose is not to eat a lot of bread, but just to taste a variety of fabulous extra virgin olive oils. Keep the practice out of your Italian restaurant experience, entirely.

# Meal Time Rules

You won't find a sit-down breakfast of eggs and bacon anywhere in Italy, outside of a hotel. But you also won't be constrained by time, if you want to eat an Italian breakfast–a *cappuccino* and a pastry–while standing up at a coffee bar. Anytime between 7am and noon will work.

The majority of eating establishments that serve lunch at the table do not start seating customers until 12:30pm. (At noon you will probably find the kitchen staff and waiters enjoying their meal.) Italians eat lunch between 12:30 and 2pm. Most will be done by 2:30pm

Most restaurants and trattorias not only have specific opening times, but you can count on them closing close in the afternoon, refusing new customers after 2:30pm. If you have a late breakfast, visit museums through lunch and hope to get a bite to eat at 2pm or 3pm, you will be eating wilted salad or dried out *panini* or worse–pre-cooked spaghetti–at a self-serve cafeteria.

Dinner is a little different. The further south you

go, the later Italians start eating. A Tuscan might consider dining at 8pm, but a Roman won't sit down before 9pm, and a Neapolitan is rarely ready to dine before 10pm. Restaurants will not start serving dinner anywhere in Italy before 7:30pm. Pizzerias start even later. But the good news is that you can stay late into the night, unlike in the U.S. or the U.K. where the owner wants to close up by 10pm.

## DID YOU KNOW?

Artisanal gelaterias are where the Italians purchase a cone of fresh-made gelato—the only kind worth eating. Because the *gelataio* is making the ice cream in the morning, the gelateria will not open before 11am. If you see gelato available for sale before 11am, you can be sure it was not made in-house. (Note also the Italian Food Rule: Italians Don't Snack. In Italy, gelato is rarely consumed before the 4pm *merenda* that helps refresh Italians so they can make it to the 8:30pm dinner hour.)

# RULES OF THE MENU

Menus in Italy are unique, uniform and sometimes a source of confusion to visitors. In no other country in the world is there such a consistent offering: *antipasti* (appetizers), *primi* (pasta, risotto and soups), *secondi* (main meat and vegetarian dishes), *contorni* (side dishes of vegetables, beans, simple salads and potatoes), and *dolce* (dessert).

Tourists frequently ask: "Do I have to order something from each section?" or "Can I get a side of pasta?" or "Why don't they bring the food we ordered all at the same time?"

Except for at special celebrations or formal dinners, Italian rarely order an *antipasto*, *primo*, *secondo*, *contorno* and *dolce* at one meal. More often they will combine a pasta and a salad and a dessert. Or they will ask for an appetizer and a main dish, perhaps followed by some fruit.

One of the Italian Food Rules holds that pasta is not a side dish. As a *primo*, it is served before the main dish, by itself. But if you only want a small portion of pasta, ask for *una mezza porzione*. You will get a half-order of pasta that will be served before the main course.

After the pasta is finished, the bowls and silverware will be replaced. A spot of pasta sauce will never touch the veal chop you ordered. Likewise, side dishes of fried potatoes or Tuscan white beans or sautéed spinach will be served on separate plates from your main dish. Think of a six-year-old in distress: "But my mashed potatoes are *touching* the fried chicken." Italians refuse to allow the flavor of one dish to invade the taste of another.

As for timing, the menu will help you to avoid the problem frequently faced by unknowing tourists when one orders a pasta and the other orders a main dish. The waiter brings the pasta first and then fifteen minutes later brings the main dish, leaving each person to eat alone as the other looks on. Solve this problem by simply asking the waiter to bring both dishes "*insieme*" (together).

Keep in mind the following: *antipasti* usually take 3 to 5 minutes to prepare; a *primo* can take up to 15 minutes (more for a risotto, but the menu will usually say so), and a *secondo* will usually take 20 minutes or more unless it is a slice off a roast, like *arista* (pork roast). So if one person wants *ravioli* (*primo*) and a salad (*contorno*), while her friend wants bruschetta (*antipasto*) and *Bistecca alla Fiorentina* (*secondo*) and they tell their waiter to bring them *insieme*, the salad and *bruschetta* will arrive first. The chef will know to put the steak on the grill before the *ravioli* go into boiling water. Just as the steak is finishing, the *ravioli* get their five minutes to cook and be sauced. Both dishes come to the table together.

The timing information inherent in the menu can also help you plan the length of a meal. In a hurry? Order a pasta and salad. Want a long relaxed meal under the stars? Savor some of the more complex dishes that you will never cook at home. Good Italian food is cooked to order from fresh ingredients. It takes time to prepare and deserves to be savored in a leisurely manner.

## DID YOU KNOW?

• A waiter will never tell you that he "needs your table".

• The check will never be placed on your table until you ask for it (unless it is after midnight).

• It will take at least 15 to 30 minutes to get your bill once you ask for it.

• Tipping is optional.

• Take twice as much time to enjoy eating a meal, as it took to cook.

• *A tavola non s'invecchia* (At the table you do not age).

# NO PIZZA FOR LUNCH

*"Mangiare la pizza prima delle nove mi fa tristezza,"* say Italians everywhere. "To eat pizza before 9pm makes me sad."

Pizza is eaten in the U.S. at any time of the day—even cold for breakfast in dorm rooms on every college campus. Italians refuse to eat food served any which way, at any time of day or night.

According to the Italian Food Rule, pizza is to be eaten at a pizzeria at night because: 1) pizza must be made to order (no frozen pizza); 2) pizza must be eaten immediately after it comes out of the pizza oven (no take-out); 3) pizza must be made by an expert—not just any old cook—a *pizzaiolo* (preferably born in Naples), who 4) is using a wood-burning pizza oven.

A wood-burning pizza oven takes a long time to get to the proper temperature (485° C or 905° F), so it will not produce the perfect pizza before 8:30 or 9 in the evening and it is usually considered a waste of time and energy (as well as a violation of the Food Rule) to fire it up for lunch. Pizzerias stay open until midnight or later, so a *pizzaiolo* gets in a full shift of work from prep at 7pm to clean-up at 1am.

Another reason for the Food Rule is that pizza, unlike pasta, is considered a social food—a food for lovers and friends—not so often for a family outing. Pasta is associated with home cooking. Traditionally, Italians were expected home for lunch for pasta. When both parents started working outside the home, the pasta meal moved to dinner.

Since the perfect pizza can't be made at home (no kitchen oven reaches 485° C and most of the private wood-burning pizza ovens built in Italy are installed at the request of foreigners who want a "true Italian experience" at their vacation villa or Tuscan farmhouse), it becomes a social event. Pizzerias provide an upbeat, carefree, casual environment where the wood-burning pizza oven is on display, as is the *pizzaiolo*, adding to the festive atmosphere.

## DID YOU KNOW?

• Eat pizza with a fork and knife (unless you are a guy *and* you are in Naples).
• Drink beer or *acqua frizzante* with pizza (Coke and Fanta, if you are under 25 years old).
• Pizza may be eaten by the slice, late at night, while standing, in a *pizza al taglio* place.
• It is sad to eat pizza alone.

# FOR PIZZA, ONE SIZE FITS ALL

Italians are not inclined to share food from plate to plate, meaning they don't take tastes, bites, or portions off each other's *pasta alle vongole* or veal chops. Therefore, there is no practice of ordering an extra large pizza for four people to share. Even two people don't share a pizza. One person, one pizza.

There are many reasons for this: hygiene, esthetics, topping choice, and pizza-eating style.

Throughout the Italian Food Rules the fear of germs is the major rationale for the rule: don't dip bread in a communal bowl of olive oil, no touching the vegetables at the market, etc. Although a shared pizza can be a virus-free act if the knife and fork skills of the participants are honed and the transfer of the slices to individual plates are handled smoothly, but then you have the problem of esthetics.

The tables in a pizzeria (you, of course, would not order a pizza anywhere else other than a pizzeria) tend to be on the small size. Therefore, a large pizza in the center of the table (displacing the candle) and individual plates in front of each diner is just not the right look, too cramped. Add beer glasses, cutlery, placemats, napkins and the condiment (*peperoncino* only) and you've got a mess. Much better to have the place settings, candle, beer, and a same-sized pizza on its own plate in front of each diner. Festive and balanced.

Probably most important reason for individual pizzas is that underlying rational of almost all Italian Food Rules—there is to be no mixing of flavors (pasta is not a side dish, no all-you-can-eat buffets, separate plates for *contorni*, etc.). Pizzas in Italy max out at about four ingredients. Even when you order a *quattro stagioni* (four seasons), each of the ingredients has its own quarter of the pizza. They do not overlap. There is no Italian pizza with "everything on it."

The pizzas described on the menu are chosen with care. The flavor meld harmoniously: *Margherita* with tomato sauce, mozzarella and one basil leaf; *Marinara* with tomato sauce, garlic and oregano; *Diavola* with tomato sauce, mozzarella and spicy salami; and *Napoletana* with tomato sauce, mozzarella, anchovies and capers, to describe a few of the classic styles. Don't ask for half *Vegetariana*, half *Diavola* or *Marinara* with mozzarella cheese (the garlic conflicts with the mozzarella). If the flavors or ingredients do not go together in any other Italian dish, they will not be considered appropriate for a pizza.

The size of an Italian pizza is time-tested and perfect for one person with little to none left over at the end (uneaten pizza is not boxed up for leftovers).

The *pizzaiolo* makes one-sized yeasty dough balls in the morning that rise during the day, perfect for making hundreds of same-sized pizzas after 8:30pm (pizza is never eaten for lunch) in a wood-burning pizza oven.

People have their own preference for how to eat their own pizza–another reason for not sharing. Some Italians, the majority, choose to eat with a knife and fork. But where one person will eat from the crust in, another might start in the center of a slice and eat out, saving the crust to last. A few Italians (men in Naples) will pick up a slice with their fingers and fold it slightly for better management while eating from the point out. Finally, a style of starting with knife and fork and savoring the last crusty bits with fingers is gaining a strong following. Can you imagine the havoc caused by two people with different pizza-eating styles sharing one pizza, even if they could agree on the toppings?

Enjoy your pizza Italian style: at night, in a pizzeria with a wood-burning pizza oven and a *pizzaiolo napoletano*, after ordering one of the classic combinations to be delivered hot on its own warm ceramic plate with a cold glass of beer. You, too, will eat the whole thing and enjoy it more than any other pizza; before or since.

# PIZZA TOPPING RULES

If you are not from Italy, you might think there are lots of condiments you can add to your pizza to make it "better." You are wrong. The only permissible condiment is hot chili flakes (*peperoncino*) to make a spicier pizza. Otherwise, leave the pizza the way the *pizzaiolo* intended it and just slice it and eat it as fast as possible. (Sometimes, hot chili flakes are not available and a *peperoncino* infused olive oil is offered as a substitute. It is not as good, but it is acceptable under the Italian Food Rules.)

Do not ask for grated Parmesan or garlic salt or salt or fresh cracked black pepper. Only hot chili flakes, nothing more.

As for any confusion about toppings—remember that Italians never eat pizza with "everything" on it. The ingredients will number four or less. Anything else is an exaggeration.

Mozzarella is the most common cheese for pizza, but it is usually used sparingly—asking for extra mozzarella will throw the texture and flavor of your pizza out of balance. Mozzarella from water buffalo (*mozzarella di bufala*) if cooked on a pizza will make it soggy; if crumbled on afterwards, it's a refreshing summer-time pizza.

If you want what is known in the U.S. as "pepperoni", ask for a *pizza con salame piccante*. "*Peperone*" in Italian is the name for bell pepper, served on *pizza vegetariana*.

There will be no pineapple in an Italian pizzeria, unless it is served, fresh-sliced, for dessert.

# DON'T PUT ICE CUBES IN BEVERAGES

Imagine you and an Italian friend are in a New York restaurant where "Hi! I'm Sam, your waiter" is assisting you to have the *best* lunch experience possible. This includes large glasses of iced water that arrive immediately on the table with a huge basket of warm bread. Guaranteed, your Italian friend will immediately start scooping out the cubes into the empty wine glass.

"Hi! I'm Sam" arrives to take your order and notices the half-full glass of iceless water. He leaves and returns with the water pitcher, which he turns sideways so that it dispenses the maximum amount of ice and a lesser amount of water. Duty done, he grins, "Now, what sounds good to you all, today?"

Italian Food Rule: No ice cubes in beverages. Ice in Italy is to keep fresh fish fresh. Full stop.

The most common reason Italians (and other Europeans) cite for the rule is that icy cold liquids are bad for your digestion. They can even cause the dreaded *congestione*–an abdominal cramp–that can kill you.

The next frequently cited reason is a fear of the tap water used for making ice. Despite the fact that Italy has very safe tap water–not always the best tasting, but safe to drink in any form–the rate of consumption of bottled water (at room temperature) in Italy is one of the highest in Europe.

No hotel in Italy will have an ice machine in the hall and few will deliver ice to the room upon request. This may be for the reasons stated above or because ice machines use a lot of very expensive electricity and are breeding grounds of all sorts of molds, fungi, and bacteria.

Italy is a land of simple drinks–wine, beer and water (*frizzante* or *naturale*)–none of which require ice. There is not a big cocktail tradition in Italy, but in a nod to the customs of the rest of the world you will frequently find three cubes of ice floating in your Negroni.

When visiting Italy, try following the Italian Food Rule: No ice cubes in beverages. You may find that you can actually taste what you are drinking.

# WITH MEALS, DRINK WATER OR WINE, NOTHING ELSE

In thousands of kitchens across America there is a person standing in front of an open fridge calling out to those gathered around the dinner table: "I've got white wine, red wine, ice tea, mango juice, beer, milk, Pellegrino, Coke, 7-Up, a bottle of Bacardi Breezer Lemon, and, of course, iced cold tap water. What does each of you want to drink?" This would never happen in an Italian kitchen.

In the homes and good restaurants of Italy the only beverages served with lunch or dinner are wine (red, white, rosé or Prosecco) and water (*frizzante* (carbonated) or *naturale* (still/no gas)). The water glasses, of course, have no ice in them.

It does not matter how young or old an Italian is: it's wine or water, only. Children sometimes have a splash of wine in their fizzy water. This practice provides them with the idea that the smart way to drink wine is in moderation.

Even adults, on a hot day, might opt for this refreshing combo by pouring a small amount of an inexpensive Chianti into a glass of ice-free *acqua frizzante*. This is not the sweet wine cooler found on picnic tables on the 4th of July. It is a sugar-free slightly flavored glass of water.

For children and adults, alike, milk is not an option (see the Italian Food Rule on drinks such as *caffellatte* and *cappuccino*). Italian mothers will tell you how milk interferes with a person's digestion.

Italians never drink coffee with food during a meal. It is sipped from tiny *espresso* cups after the last bite is swallowed. Don't try to tempt an Italian with an extra morsel after the espresso is served. (It's sort of the same as offering an American a cookie after they've brushed their teeth.) Also, coffee is never drunk *throughout* the meal in Italy because it too interferes with digestion—in an acidic way, rather than a curdling way—any Italian grandmother will tell you. However, the same *nonna* will also tell you that a shot of espresso at the end of the meal aids in digestion.

Juices, sodas, cocktails, and even sugarless ice tea all interfere with the flavor of the food. To savor the true taste of each ingredient is of utmost importance to Italians, as well as those who truly love Italian cooking. The only beverages that complement Italian cuisine are wine and water.

"But what about beer?" you might ask. Until recently, Italy did not have a rich beer tradition, but Peroni and Moretti have been around since the middle of the 1800's. Italians drink beer with pizza. This does not violate the Italian Food Rule: Wine or Water, Nothing Else, because pizza is not a meal. Pizza is...well...*pizza*. Neither wine nor water complement pizza as well as beer does. Kids and teenagers celebrate the lifting of the "no sodas" ban on pizza nights.

Then the next day it's back to wine or water, nothing else.

## DID YOU KNOW?

It is bad luck to toast each other at the table with anything but wine.

# Rules For Drinking Wine

To Italians, wine and food go together. It is a marriage. Divorcing the two is next to impossible in Italy. You will never be invited to an Italian's home for drinks. You will not be offered a glass of wine after you take your coat off and before you sit down to eat, unless a full platter of appetizers makes its appearance first.

In a restaurant, you will not be asked what you want to drink before you order your meal. If the waiter offers you a glass of Prosecco before you order, you know two things: 1) the restaurant serves a lot of tourists; and 2) a complimentary appetizer will come with the spritzy white wine. If the bottle of wine you ordered with your meal arrives on the table before the food, the Italians at the table will not drink until at least the *antipasti* are served. They may not drink wine until they get to the main course.

A couple of years ago, a survey of over 800 American wine drinkers came up with the result that only 41 percent of the wine drunk was consumed while sitting down to a meal. Nineteen percent was consumed with appetizers and snack food (nuts, chips, etc.), and 14 percent was sipped in the kitchen while preparing food (so perhaps a taste of food, here or there). That means 26 percent of wine, consumed by Americans who profess to love the beverage, was drunk without food at all.

Perhaps Italians understand that the natural acidity of wine begs for food. It is assumed that the purpose of wine always is to accompany and enhance foods. And, more importantly, food enhances the flavor of wine. Where the tannins in wine dry out the mouth and impart a slightly bitter flavor, food stimulates the salivary glands and brings a more rounded taste to wine.

Italians are rarely pretentious about their wine choices or their wine/food pairing. The whole issue of choosing the "right" wine for a certain dish came from the fussy French and was copied by Americans who wished to show off their culinary acumen.

Italians tend to be regional in their wine selection. When in Rome, eating a Roman dish *Bucatini all'Amatriciana* or *Baccalà alla Trasteverina,* the wine selection will probably be a refreshing white from the Frascati wine-growing region on one of the "seven hills" just south of Rome. If the truffled dishes of Piemonte are served in Torino, a Barolo or Barbaresco, made from the local Nebbiolo grape, will be ordered. Although a Roman might on occasion order a Tuscan Chianti Classico, a Piemontese would never consider doing the same, unless he was dining in Siena. You will rarely see wines from France, Spain or the U.S. on an Italian wine list, unless you are in an ostentatious restaurant.

*Vino della Casa*, the house wine, will be local and, with very few exceptions, will taste great. It will complement the local food, but will not be a wine you would want to drink on its own. Italians don't. In regions where the local food does not go with white wine, such as Tuscany, you will rarely find a white house wine. In Venice, with its famous creamy *Baccalà Mantecato* and tapas-portioned *cicchetti*, the house wine will be a bubbly white Prosecco or cold Soave from the Veneto.

Glassware will range from small squat glasses used for both water and house wine, to standard generic stemmed glasses, great for most every Italian wine, to fine crystal stemware chosen to complement the aroma and taste of a fine Brunello. They all work for Italians. Again, they leave the pretentious glassware choices to the French and the Americans.

Most important—even though he was French—the Italians will agree with Andrè Simon (1877-1970), a wine merchant, gourmet, and prolific writer about wine, when he wrote, "Food without wine is a corpse; wine without food is a ghost; united and well matched they are as body and soul, living partners." But they will also concur with their own Tuscan Galileo Galilei, who said, "Wine is sunlight, held together by water."

# "SUPER TUSCAN" IS NOT ITALIAN

"Bring me one of those Super Tuscans, please," requests a tourist from San Francisco to the Roman waiter in an up-scale restaurant. "Something with cabernet sauvignon or merlot in it." The waiter will probably not be confused by the order of a Super Tuscan, but he will more likely bring the wine list than make a selection for his customer.

Although today the moniker "Super Tuscan" is universally used by Americans to denote a wide variety of fine red wines from Tuscany, the expression was originally adopted by English-language wine writers as an unofficial descriptor to describe high quality wines that had been classified by the Italian government as *vino da tavola* (table wine). The Italians have never used the term and there is no comparable phrase in the Italian language today.

No one really knows who coined the term "Super Tuscan," although many believe that the designation was first used by writer Burton Anderson, who covered Italy for *Wine Spectator* in the 1980s. This English term "Super Tuscan" came to stand for winemaking that dared to defy tradition and break the rules.

It is easy to imagine in 1971, Anderson was sipping a great glass of Tignanello, a cabernet sauvignon/cabernet franc/sangiovese blend, with its creator Marchese Piero Antinori, listening to the vintner complain about the fact that he couldn't get the Americans to pay the price the wine deserved. "It's all in the marketing," Anderson might have said. "You need a good catch phrase. How about 'Super Tuscan'?"

The term "Super Tuscan" describes any Tuscan red wine that does not adhere to traditional blending laws for the region. For example, Chianti Classico DOCG wines are made from a blend of grapes with Sangiovese as the dominant variety (at least 80 %) in the blend. If the winery doesn't follow the recipe, it doesn't get to use the designation.

Super Tuscans often contain grapes that were not traditionally grown in Italy, such as cabernet sauvignon, cabernet franc, merlot or syrah, making them ineligible for DOC(G) classification under the traditional rules.

In 1992, Italian authorities came up with a new category, *Indicazione Geografica Tipica* (IGT) that designates a geographic area, while giving wide latitude in winemaking. Many Super Tuscans today fall under this designation. While still a potent marketing device, the rubric "Super Tuscan" has become a sort of catchall for the pricier red wines of the region that don't follow the DOC(G) classifications.

If you want to discuss fine wine with an Italian, leave out the term "Super Tuscan" and start by using the IGT designation and then perhaps, talk about *vino particolare,* a good Italian term for an IGT wine that is particular, special or even, super.

## DID YOU KNOW?

Although many Tuscan vintners wish the claim to fame of being the creator of the first Super Tuscan, most would agree that this credit belongs to Marchese Mario Incisa della Rocchetta and his wine Sassicaia, made from Cabernet Sauvignon at his Tenuta San Guido estate in Bolgheri. In 1950, he started making wine with French grapes using Italian methods. At its inception, Sassicaia was the family's personal wine. The 1968 vintage was released commercially after 1970 when the famous enologist, Giacomo Tachis, was brought on to make Sassicaia the full-bodied wine it is today.

The problem for these innovative vintners was that if they did not qualify for the DOC or DOCG designations, they were required to label their wine *Vino Rosso da Tavola* (Red Table Wine), a term usually applied low quality wines, and no one wanted to pay a high price for plain old red table wine, especially the Americans.

In the 1970s, Marchese Piero Antinori, whose family had been making wine for more than 700 years, and was related to Marchese Incisa della Rocchetta, also decided to make a more complex wine that could tolerate aging by eliminating the then mandated white grapes from the Chianti blend, and instead added Bordeaux varietals (namely, Cabernet Sauvignon and Cabernet Franc). The resulting wine did not qualify for the Chianti Classico DOC. It was mere red table wine.

What was formerly Chianti Classico Riserva Vigneto Tignanello, denied the DOC designation as a Chianti Classico wine in 1971 because Antinori refused to use white grapes in the blend, became simply Tignanello (after the name of the vineyard), the second Super Tuscan, after its cousin Sassicaia.

# No Butter For the Bread

"Where's the butter for the bread?" asks a tourist from Chicago. "Can we get some butter out here?" asks a lady from Atlanta.

"*Perché?*" queries the waiter. *Perché?* indeed. In Italy, bread is not better with butter. Butter never meets bread on the Italian peninsula, except for a breakfast of a slice of toast with butter and *marmellata* or an after-school snack of bread, butter, and sugar or bread, butter and anchovies.

At lunch or dinner, Italians wouldn't think of spreading butter on the bread from the basket on the table. In fact, bread is served with the meal solely for the purpose of acting as the *scarpetta* - the little shoe. Italians say, "*fare la scarpetta*" to mean use as a little shoe of bread to scoop up the last remnants of sauce on the plate.

To ask for butter in a restaurant, or a family home, puts the host in a quandary. The kitchen may have a quarter kilo or more of butter, but it isn't table-worthy. There are no cute pats of butter or, even, butter dishes in restaurants or most homes.

When you visit Italy, give up bread and butter for the duration of your stay—you and your waistline will appreciate it—and think how good it will taste when you get home.

## DID YOU KNOW?

Toasted bread slathered with butter and sprinkled with garlic salt is *not* Italian Garlic Bread. Make *fettunta* (known as *bruschetta* outside Tuscany)—slices of hot toasted Tuscan bread, rubbed with a clove of fresh garlic, splashed with fresh extra virgin olive oil and sprinkled with salt.

# DANTE LOVED BREAD MADE WITHOUT SALT

Tourists are frequently surprised when they first taste traditional Tuscan bread that is always made without salt. Tuscans, especially Florentines, would not eat it any other way.

Dante agreed. *"Tu proverai sí come sa di sale lo pane altrui, e come è duro calle lo scendere e 'l salir per l'altrui scale."* In these lines from the *Paradiso* of "The Divine Comedy," Dante learns of his exile from Florence and is given some idea of the difficulties he will face. "You shall learn how salty is the taste of another's bread, and how hard a path the descending and the climbing another's stairs," he is told by Cacciaguida.

The Pisans get all the blame from some pundits for the bland bread made by the Florentines. Supposedly, they attempted to force Florence to surrender in one of their endless battles against each other by blockading the salt that arrived at the Pisan port, preventing it from reaching Florence via the Arno River.

Others claim that the widespread poverty in the

Middle Ages is to blame when salt was too costly for the Tuscans to use in bread-making. (It's hard to credit this story because poor Italian peasants in other regions couldn't afford salt, but didn't give up making salted bread.)

I like to think it was the pope's fault. During the 14th to 16th centuries, it is said, the popes, who controlled much of the Italian peninsula (known as the Papal States), levied a tax on salt. Pope Paul III raised the tax in 1539 and the Perugians and the Tuscans refused to pay it. The government of Perugia even went to war over the issue–the Salt War of 1540. The Perugians lost the war, but some say the citizens then refused to buy the salt, thus forcing the *fornai* (bread bakeries) to produce salt-free bread. (Tuscan bread is one of the few that remains salt-free today, but there are many historical references to bread made without salt in other parts of Italy.)

During the 16th century in Tuscany, the Tuscan Medici dukes controlled all of the resources of the region, including salt. When they needed cash (for a war or for building a new villa) they raised the price on salt and other commodities. Thus, *pane toscano* (Tuscan bread) became bread famous throughout Italy for being *sciocco*, from the word in the Tuscan dialect for "insipid" (to Tuscans "*sciocco*" also means "stupid", but that doesn't fit this situation because they think salt-less bread is anything, but stupid). Those who are not Tuscan make fun of the bread of the region, but Tuscans, like Dante, mourn the loss of it when they travel.

Salt-less Tuscan bread is not intended for eating on its own. It's usually served along with the main meal and is meant for sopping up thick, rich, spicy sauces. The bread doesn't compete with the flavors in the dish; both are enhanced.

Tuscan bread has a rustic look with a crunchy crust. The soft middle part of the loaf is honey-combed in appearance. Its lack of salt helps keep it fresh for several days. Since it has no salt to hold in water, it does not form mold–it just becomes hard as a rock when it is stale–thus making it the basis of many of the tasty dishes that are renowned in Tuscan cuisine.

# DID YOU KNOW?

The following Italian dishes are made with stale salt-free Tuscan bread:

*Ribollita*–a twice-boiled thick vegetable soup (*ribollita* means 're-boiled'), made of black and white cabbage, white beans and other vegetables, made thick with crumbled stale Tuscan bread or poured over toasted Tuscan bread.

*Pappa al pomodoro*–a bread-based thick tomato soup in which stale Tuscan bread is rehydrated and crumbled; then cooked with the tomatoes, basil and garlic to make a tasty *pappa*.

*Panzanella*–a summer salad dish. Stale Tuscan bread is soaked in water, squeezed into a damp mass, crumbled into a big salad bowl and cucumber, raw onion, fresh diced tomato and fresh basil leaves are added. The ingredients are tossed thoroughly with some extra virgin olive oil, salt and pepper.

*Cacciucco*–a fish chowder from Livorno made of fish, mollusks and crustaceans. The Livornese claim that the recipe should contain at least five types of fish to match the number of 'c's in the word *cacciucco*. Once cooked, the *cacciucco* is served on a bed of toasted Tuscan bread that has been rubbed with a clove of fresh garlic.

*Fettunta/Bruschetta*–"garlic toast" made with slices of hot toasted Tuscan bread, rubbed with a clove of fresh garlic, splashed with fresh extra virgin olive oil and sprinkled with salt. Don't try to cut into a completely stale loaf of Tuscan bread to make this; it's too hard to cut. Use slightly stale bread–too dry to eat untoasted, but perfect for *fettunta* or *bruschetta*.

# LARD IS LUSCIOUS

Place a platter with a large rectangle of lard on the table, pass around a basket of warm toasted Tuscan bread slices, and you have a contented table of Italians. *Lardo di Colonnata* is delectable and has been an Italian traditional dish since before the time of Michelangelo.

*Lardo* is pork fatback and is 100% fat. Most Americans squirm at the idea of eating pure fat, and pig fat, at that. But olive oil is also 100% fat. Lard (*lardo*) is lower in saturated fat and cholesterol, and higher in mono- and poly-unsaturated fats than butter. Lard and butter aren't public enemy No. 1 anymore. Instead the hydrogenated fats–margarine, for instance, the so-called "healthy" fat of the 1970's–have turned out to be the "bad" fats.

For over one thousand years, *lardo* has been made in the same way in Colonnata, near Carrara. The marble quarrymen used to take a big slice of lard and a few dried tomatoes, wrapped in a hunk of bread, off to work each day. The high caloric sandwich would carry them through the long hours of hard labor.

The process for making *lardo* is complex. It starts in the fall when pigs of at least nine months of age and weighing over 350 pounds are butchered. Rectangular strips of fatback, each at least one and quarter inch thick, are cut. The maturation takes place in marble tubs (*le conche di marmo*) placed in caves or cool cellars. To give the lard its unique flavor the tubs are rubbed with garlic and the lard is immersed in brine. Sea salt mixed with spices and herbs (always rosemary, peppercorns, and garlic, but sometimes including anise seed, thyme, oregano, sage, nutmeg, and cloves) is rubbed over each slab in a thick layer. The strips are fit, puzzle-like, layer upon layer in the marble casks, repeating the process over and over. Once the tub is full, it is covered with a wooden lid or a marble cover. The curing time runs from a minimum of six months to one year.

*Lardo di Colonnata* is white with a pink streak. Thanks to the particular maturation procedure, the Lard of Colonnata is a natural product, free from preservatives and coloring. The best way to eat this lard is on toasted bread or on polenta, laying a paper-thin slice of room temperature *lardo* on the still warm bread or polenta. For a savory-sweet treat, dot sliced *lardo* with fig preserves or *mostarda di frutta* (an Italian condiment made with candied fruit and powdered mustard). Let the *lardo* melt on your tongue followed by the sweet taste with the mustard kick. Despite the amount of salt used in curing the fatback, *lardo* is surprisingly mild.

Next time the mixed appetizers (*crostini misti*) are passed, grab the small toast with the translucent fold of *lardo* melting on top before the Italians do. You will be in for a flavor treat.

# DID YOU KNOW?

Despite its centuries-long history, the most eventful times for *lardo* have been recent. In April 1996, the powers-that-be realized that no *lardarium* had ever been inspected or authorized by the regional boards of health. European Union food inspectors got involved. Countless *conche di marmo* were sealed and several hundred pounds of lard were confiscated from Colonnata's dirt-floored cellars and caves. The resulting analysis revealed that all samples tested were found beyond reproach and it was proven once and for all that the use of marble containers posed no health threat.

Despite the laboratory findings, however, producers were ordered to meet existing health practices, including using preservatives and disposable plastic tubs, tiling the cellars, forbidding use of the caves for aging–essentially bankrupting the *lardarium* system.

The EU's action caused a grass-roots movement that led to *Lardo di Colonnata* becoming one of the first traditional Italian foods, made using many of the ancient methods, to be protected under the Arca del Gusto di Slow Food, supported by the Slow Food Italia organization, *Provincia di Massa Carrara* and the

*Regione Toscana.* Twelve of the fourteen producers were able to remain in business.

To make sure they are getting traditionally made *lardo*, Italians ask to see the IGP (*Indicazione Geografica Protetta*) brand on the rind or the DOP (*Denominazione di Origine Protetta*).

Other regions produce tasty *lardo*, including:

1) *Lardo di Arnad*, once made in oak casks and now aged in steel containers, comes from Valle d'Aosta. It is sometimes stored thereafter in glass jars, covered with white wine.

2) From Cavour, a small town in the Piemonte region, a famous butcher, Silvio Brarda, produces a special rosemary-infused *lardo, Lardo al rosmarino di Cavour.*

3) Another Tuscan *lardo* is produced near Florence in the town of Greve. *Lardo Val di Greve*, made from special mature *Cinta Senese* pigs, is known for its reasonable price and delicate flavor.

# PASTA IS NOT A SIDE DISH

For Italians pasta is a dish to be revered on its own, not shoved onto a plate beside some more important entrée.

Pasta is a *primo*–among the first dishes. It is to be served separately in its own bowl. The flavors of the pasta noodle and the accompanying sauce are to be savored without any other food–no bread, no vegetables, no meat or fish. Nothing should interfere with the enjoyment of a dish of pasta, properly sauced.

In fact, Italians will take care in telling you that it is "pasta with sauce" not "sauce with pasta". It is important that a light hand adds the sauce so that the flavor of the pasta noodle itself is not overwhelmed or covered up.

Once the pasta noodles are all gone, the small amount of remaining sauce can be captured and enjoyed by employing a small torn piece of bread, just big enough for one bite.

# PASTA IS COOKED *AL DENTE*

In the '80s every want-to-be cook in America got a fresh pasta-making machine and at least once or twice made fresh pasta. The results were usually disappointing and the biggest problem was the resulting mushy, gummy pasta. There was frequently something wrong with the dough, but more often the fresh pasta was cooked much too long.

Italians know that the best pasta has some "chew" to it–pasta cooked *al dente* (literally "at the tooth"). Italians also know that it is next to impossible to achieve this texture with fresh pasta. The cooking time is usually about one to three minutes long and must be stopped somehow after the pasta is removed from boiling water.

Dried pasta is the answer. Americans seem to think that dried pasta is bad or old pasta (and frequently what Americans find on their grocery shelves fits those descriptions). Italians know that dried pasta, made by a reputable company, is flavorful and cooks up perfectly.

Dried pasta takes up to nine to eighteen minutes

to cook properly, depending on the type of flour and the shape. The key is to get the center of the noodle to cook through (losing the telltale white spot and the tiny crunch when it is bitten) and then stop the cooking process immediately by removing the pasta from the boiling water, not just turning the heat off under the pot.

For some sauces it is best to take the pasta up to the last couple of minutes, drain it and then sauté it in the sauce for the final two minutes, thereby adding more flavor to the noodles.

Have you heard that old wives tale–throw the pasta against the wall–if it sticks, it's done? It's a sure fire way to make your kitchen wall a disgusting mess. The more pasta cooks, the gummier it gets, so if it sticks to the wall it's overdone. The only way to know if it's properly cooked is to bite it. It should be *al dente*, or firm to the bite, but not crunchy.

Did your favorite aunt rinse pasta after cooking and draining so it wouldn't stick together? This will make the pasta cold and rinse away the starch that helps bind the sauce to it. If it sticks together, it's overcooked. Or did she add olive oil to the cooking water to keep the pasta from sticking? Pasta shouldn't stick when properly cooked. If it's cooked with olive oil, the noodles will be coated and prevent the tasty sauce from sticking. The only ingredient to be added to the pasta water just as it starts to boil, before dropping in the dry noodles, is a small hand-ful of large grain sea salt (or about 2 tablespoons of regular salt).

There are two cases where Italians demand fresh pasta. First, filled pastas, like *ravioli* or *tortellini*, where the filling must be fresh, not dried, must have fresh pasta to hold the filling inside. In this case, the cooking time is usually about three to five minutes and the pasta should still be *al dente*.

Second, fresh *tagliatelle*, usually bright yellow from the egg yokes in the pasta dough, is also a fresh-made pasta loved especially by northern Italians. It cooks up in two to three minutes (*al dente*, again) and calls for a delicate topping like butter and shaved white truffles. (For those on a budget, salt-free creamy butter and fresh cracked black pepper is almost as good.)

Italians will tell you that with food it isn't just the taste; it isn't just the look; it isn't just the aroma; it is also the texture that is important. Give your pasta some "chew."

# SPAGHETTI IS NOT SERVED WITH MEATBALLS

"Mamma mia, thatsa spicy meatball," the red-faced "Italian" man said each time his stereotypical wife plunked down a steaming plate of spaghetti and meatballs...until the antacid commercial hit its punchline. "Spaghetti and meatballs, now that's Italian!" is found in the script of many a B-movie. Even Lady and the Tramp have their first kiss over spaghetti and meatballs served up by Tony, the mustachioed Italian singing cook, in the 1955 movie.

The Italian Food Rule holds that there will be no meatballs on top of spaghetti. Spaghetti with meatballs is not an authentic Italian dish. (To find "spaghetti with meatballs" on a menu anywhere in Italy means that you are eating in a tourist trap.)

If you inquire about the dish in Italy, your waiter may laugh, but more likely sneer. If pasta and meatballs are served in the same meal, the two ingredients will be served separately–the spaghetti as a *primo* and the meatballs (*polpette*) as a *secondo*.

Spaghetti served with "red sauce" and topped

with meatballs is an American creation. The pasta recipe probably made its first appearance in New York or New Jersey in the late 1800s, most likely as a reaction to the socio-economic conditions experienced by a wave of Italian immigrants who arrived at the turn of the 20th century. They left Italy poor and started lives in America poor. Meat was costly. For special occasions, when meat was served, the portions were small–too embarrassing to offer alone on the plate. But as a topping for cheap pasta and thin tomato sauce, meatballs the size of walnuts made the platter a celebration.

In the 1930s, the jolly Chef Boyardee was celebrated from coast to coast for his spaghetti with meatballs. Ettore Boiardi left Piacenza in 1915 at age 17 to land a job in the kitchen at the Plaza Hotel in NYC. By 1928, he had invented a meatball-making machine. Like Tony in the Lady and the Tramp, Ettore (soon known as Hector) liked the spicy meatballs and he put them in a can with spaghetti, ready to be opened at every American kid's lunch. No child in Italy will ever see spaghetti with meatballs for lunch or dinner.

Of course, with prosperity came exaggeration. The platter of pasta was the same size, but the sauce became thicker, drowning the spaghetti, and the meatballs grew to the size of a child's fist.

The Italian-American spaghetti and meatball myth always invokes grandma's recipe. Marcella Hazan, the true expert on how Americans should prepare authentic Italian food, agreed with the Italian

Food Rule. For those in search of the same flavor, she endorses a fine recipe for pasta with a meat sauce (*ragù*), but nixed untidy balls of meat that roll down a heap of over-cooked spaghetti.

# DID YOU KNOW?

• Alfredo is a man's name not a pasta sauce–ask for pasta with a sauce containing *panna* (cream).

• Bolognese is a descriptive term–ask for *ragù alla Bolognese* for the rich meat sauce.

• You must pair the correct shape of pasta with the correct sauce–long pasta (*spaghetti, tagliatelle*) with to-mato and smooth sauces and short pasta (*penne, riga-toni*) with chunky sauces.

• Pasta salads are not made with fresh pasta or long pasta or mayonnaise.

• Do not cut your spaghetti–twirl it on a fork against the edge of the bowl, unless you are less than ten years old, when you can use a spoon to help twirl the noodles.

• Pasta is never served with a sauce made with chicken or rabbit, but you might find a tasty *pap-pardelle sulla lepre* (wide pasta with wild hare sauce).

# DON'T EAT BREAD WITH PASTA

Bread is not eaten with pasta in Italy. Bread accompanies the *secondo* (main dish), not the *primo piatto* (pasta course). The primary reason for this Italian Food Rule is that bread with pasta constitutes two starches being eaten together, each interfering with the taste of the other.

Many times bread is more of a utensil than a food. A small piece torn off a slice of bread–*scarpetta*–may be eaten after the pasta is finished to mop up those last traces of sauce that can't be caught by the fork.

*Scarpetta* means "little shoe" in Italian. *Fare la scarpetta*–do the little shoe–happens after every last pasta noodle has been eaten and traces of delicious sauce are still in the bowl. A person simply takes a piece of bread from the basket, tears off the appropriate sized piece, pinches an edge and scoops the sauce. That piece of bread transforms into a tiny shoe and the sauce is the slippery ground across which your little shoe is sliding, the sole picking up traces as it goes.

Tuscan bread, made with no salt, has little taste of its own so it is the perfect bread to *fare la scarpetta*, especially with spicy sauces.

Italians can be divided into two groups: those who do the *scarpetta*, and those few who don't. Some people do so only furtively because their mothers told them it was not good manners. More brazen food lovers just dig in with no regrets. A good *scarpettaro* will leave the plate with no trace of sauce.

# Don't Eat Cheese With Fish

Nothing is more likely to raise the ire of your Italian waiter than to ask for some grated parmesan to go on your *spaghetti alle vongole* or *pasta al baccalà*. The reasons for the Food Rule are: logic, location, and tradition.

Except for salt cod (*baccalà*), canned tuna, cured sardines and anchovies (*acciughe*), Italians believe fish should be eaten fresh, close to the place and time that it is caught. Fish from the seas and rivers of Italy is mild tasting, delicate, and needs to be treated with a light touch when it comes to seasoning. The milky saltiness of cheese will overwhelm the flavor of the fish. And fishy cheese is just hard to contemplate, much less swallow.

Italian cheese producing regions tend to be inland and landlocked: parmesan in the north, pecorino in the hills of Tuscany, and buffalo mozzarella to the east and south of Naples. Famed for fish are the Ligurian, Sicilian, Adriatic and Tuscan coastal towns. Italians have been living the Slow Food, zero kilometer lifestyle for centuries. The recipes celebrate the location and availability of fresh ingredients: where there is fish there isn't cheese, and vice versa.

Location and tradition meet in the recipes passed down for generations. Italians don't move far from their places of birth and those places were city-states just 150 years ago. In Livorno, they argue over the types of shellfish and saltwater fish that should go into *cacciucco* (cheese never enters the discussion). In Bologna chefs add more cheese on top of a cheesy sauce covering ravioli stuffed with cheese, but not one thinks of filling his ravioli with fish. For centuries, tradition dictated that meat and dairy products were forbidden on Friday for religious reasons. Fish was the symbolic and nutritional replacement, but heaven forbade a topping of cheese.

Caveat: The wry Robert Trachtenberg, writing "Just Grate" in the *NY Times*, found the oldest surviving "Sicilian recipe–from around 400 B.C.–for fish: 'Gut. Discard the head, rinse, slice; add cheese and oil.'" Trachtenberg also browbeat famous chefs in Rome and Venice until they admitted to serving fish pastas with cheese added in the kitchen.

## DID YOU KNOW?

- Cheese does not go with garlic and oil-based pasta sauces.
- Spicy cheeses (pecorino) go on spicy dishes.
- Don't add cheese–grated or cubed–to salads.

• Caprese (mozzarella, tomato, and basil) is not a salad; it's an *antipasto* or a *secondo*.

• Breaded meats and poultry do not get sprinkled with Parmesan cheese (chicken parmigiana or veal parmigiana are not Italian) or buried under a blanket of mozzarella.

# DON'T EAT EGGS IN THE MORNING

There is a reason that it is called an American Breakfast or an English Breakfast. If it contains eggs, it is not Italian. Italians are most likely to have a cappuccino and a pastry for the "most important meal of the day." They might stretch to a small bowl of yogurt and a half piece of fruit. But eggs are out.

In Italy, eggs are usually eaten hard-boiled, sliced in half (not crumbled) beside (not in) a lunchtime salad. Or, more commonly, they are prepared as a *frittata* (thin open-faced omelet) containing a few slices of artichoke, zucchini, eggplant or fried green tomatoes.

For dinner at home, Tuscans enjoy a savory dish of *uova al pomodoro* (eggs cooked in tomatoes) that consists of eggs sunny-side-up (one per person) cooked directly on a bed of chunky stewed fresh tomatoes, flavored with a bit of garlic, fresh basil and olive oil. Some crusty bread finishes the meal.

# Did You Know?

- Orange juice is too acidic to drink in the morning.
- Bacon is *becon* or *pancetta affumicata* in Italy and is not seen at breakfast, but may be in *spaghetti alla carbonara*.
- Pancakes and waffles are loved by Italians, but are not Italian.
- Italians don't understand the concept of "breakfast for dinner."

# BISTECCA ALLA FIORENTINA IS ALWAYS SERVED RARE

*Bistecca alla Fiorentina* (beefsteak Florentine style) must be served rare. Don't ask for it well done or, even, medium. It has very little fat marbling, so it gets tough when it is cooked too long.

This Tuscan steak is comparable to a T-Bone or porterhouse cut. It is the flavorful meat of the white, long-legged, grass-fed Chianina cattle.

The Chianina breed originate in the area of the Val di Chiana, are the tallest and heaviest breed in the world and one of the oldest, having been raised in Italy for at least 2000 years (the first written accounts appears in 55 AD).

Bistecca alla Fiorentina is never slathered with barbeque sauce, either during the grilling or after. Typically weighing in at one kilo (2.2 pounds), the steaks are grilled over a charcoal fire (5 minutes on each side and 15 minutes standing on end on the bone), and then seasoned with salt, black pepper, and perhaps, a splash (after the steak is removed from the fire) of olive oil. *Bistecca* is frequently garnished with a lemon wedge. It's okay to share one steak for two. Don't ask for steak sauce or a pat of butter.

If cooked properly, *Bistecca alla Fiorentina* will be tender enough to cut with a table knife. If it's cooked too long it will be as tough as shoe leather. If your chef agrees to cook a Chianina beefsteak to medium or well done, he isn't Italian or you are eating in a tourist trap.

# DON'T PASS THE GRAVY

Gravy–all those meaty drippings, fats, flour and other thickeners, and, perhaps, a hunk of butter– what's not to like? It's good on everything from meat, poultry (especially turkey), mashed or stir-fried potatoes, cornbread, grits, to good old buttermilk biscuits. Gravy ties the meal together. Sometimes, gravy is the main ingredient of a meal.

For Italians, that's just the problem. In Italy, different dishes are meant to be on...well...*different* dishes. In other words, the potatoes, either mashed or oven-roasted, are served on a separate plate than the *ossobuco*. Each food, made with its own special recipe, is meant to be savored separately, so that you can taste each ingredient the cook used.

The *ossobuco* may have some pan drippings around it, but those savory drips are not to touch the sweet spring peas that have been steamed with only a couple of whole cloves (not crushed) of garlic and a sprig or two of parsley. The peas, a *contorno* (side dish), are to be served to you on a separate plate. You are to eat them from that plate and not transfer them to your *secondo* (the main dish, the *ossobuco*) to let them roll them around in the meat sauce.

Gravy, by its very nature, is meant to tie diverse foods together in a, hopefully, harmonious taste. Italian menus are created with care so that the pairing of the dishes is harmonious without having to be bound together by a saucy tsunami of gravy.

# TRIPE IS TASTY TO TUSCANS

Tripe (*trippa*) is what Americans coyly refer to as "variety meats" and what some Italian aficionados sometimes call the *quinto quarto* (fifth quarter) of the animal. Usually it refers to the lining of one of the four chambers of a ruminant's stomach, usually a young ox. But a *trippaio* (tripe butcher) will sell the bits and pieces of the *quinto quarto* of veal, beef, and pork. Italians, especially Florentines, swear that *trippa* is one of the Italian delicacies that doesn't get enough attention.

When properly cooked, Italians claim these meats are delicious–tender, mild yet flavorful, without being overtly fatty.

*Trippa alla fiorentina* is the white honey comb muscle of the cow's second stomach cooked in a rich tomato sauce, but the classic is the *panino col lampredotto*–long-simmered, light purple-brown from the cow's fourth stomach served as a sandwich at lunchtime with either a *salsa piccante* (hot chili flakes and olive oil) and/or a *salsa verde* (parsley, capers, garlic and anchovies, among other ingredients)–it's called *completo* when you want both sauces—at one of the specialist *trippaio* carts parked on sidewalks and in piazzas. (Florence boasts of nine tripe stands, one for each neighborhood in the historic center of the city, and 23 more in the periphery of the city.)

The true skill, learned young, is how to eat this soggy sandwich (*panino col lampredotto*), with its saucy meat and bread that has been quickly dunked in the meat juice, without getting it on your shirt or tie. The "lampredotto lean" (kind of like the Tower of Pisa) creates the right angle, but you still need plenty of napkins to wipe your chin.

For a change, an Italian might ask for *poppa* (udder—cooked for nearly eight hours to melting tenderness) on toasted bread or *nervetti* (tendons—more texture than flavor) cooked in tomato sauce. In Rome, intestines from milk-fed calf or lamb are used to make *pajata*. In Sicily the same are grilled and sold on the streets—*stigghiole* is what you need to ask for if you want to try them.

The home cook will stop by a favorite *trippaio* in the market and find creamy white or russet mats of raw tripe from all four chambers of the cow's stomach, dominating the glassed-in counter, accompanied by ears, hoofs, cheeks, muzzles, testicles, udders, kidneys and other internal and external body parts of pork, veal and beef. Although you will probably not be served tripe as a dinner guest in an Italian home, the number of *trippai* doing good business in the Italian food markets show that tripe is being dished out at many an Italian family lunch table.

Try a *mezza porzione* (half portion) at your favorite trattoria next time you want to be Italian for a day.

# THEY EAT HORSES, DON'T THEY?

In Europe and Japan, it is a staple, and in Sweden horse meat outsells mutton and lamb combined. Residents of Austria, Belgium, Canada, Chile, China, France, Germany, Iceland, Indonesia, Kazakhstan, Malta, Mongolia, the Netherlands, Norway, Poland, Slovenia, and Switzerland all consume horse meat. But Italy surpasses all other countries in the European Union in horse meat consumption.

The meat itself is similar to beef, although many say it is slightly sweeter in taste (somewhere between beef and venison) and has a less complex flavor. That said, many Italians argue that it is a healthier option than beef, being both lower in fat and having a higher content of protein, iron, Omega-3, Vitamin B-12 and glycogen.

It is an inexpensive meat and it used to be the red meat for the poor, but now is consumed by all economic classes. One reason for the increased consumption came about 10 years ago with the fears of BSE (mad cow disease) in beef. The disease is not found in horses.

Don't worry if you are afraid that you might not recognize the difference between horse and beef in the market. In 1928, Italian legislation was passed to prohibit the sale of horse meat together with other meats in the same stores. In the big food markets, horse meat is sold at a specialty stand by specialist horse butchers. The Roman Catholic Church prohibited eating horse meat in the 8th century, and the taboo still remains, but is not followed by many Catholic Italians. On a menu, keep an eye out for the words *cavallo* or *carne equina*, and in Sardinia the dialect word for horse is *cuaddu*.

Horse meat is used in a variety of Italian recipes: as a stew called *pastissada* (typical of Verona), served as steaks, as *carpaccio* (raw), or made into *bresaola* (cured). Even classic Italian *mortadella* sausage can be had in a horse meat variety. Minute shredded strips of salted, dried and smoked horse meat called *sfilacci* are popular in the Veneto region. A long-cooked stew called *pezzetti di cavallo* combines cubed horse meat with tomato sauce, onions, carrots and celery. Horse meat sausages (*salsiccia di equino*) and salamis are traditional in northern Italy. In Sardinia, *sa petza 'e cuaddu* is one of the most popular meats and sometimes is sold in typical kiosks with bread. Donkey is also cooked, for example as a stew called *stracotto d'asino* and as meat for sausages e.g. *mortadella d'asino*. The cuisine of Parma features a horsemeat tartare, called *pesto di cavallo,* marinated in lemon juice with fresh garlic and chopped parsley.

Visitors to the north and south of Italy will have many chances to try horse meat, if they are so inclined. It's a regional Italian food that a tradition going back centuries.

## DID YOU KNOW?

Today, in Tuscany, consumption of horse meat is rare, although there is one stand, Pica Nicolino Elena, in the *Mercato Centrale* of Florence where specialty horse butcher Nicola Ricci has sold a wide variety of products for decades, as did his father before him. There used to be five stands in the market selling horse meat. Florence has a couple of restaurants that offers a horse steak and Da Giulio, a trattoria in Lucca, regularly has a popular dish of marinated raw *cavallo alla tartara* on the menu.

# *BACCALÀ* BINDS AND DIVIDES ITALY

In the U.S. you can count on finding a burger at every truck stop, small town or major city. In the U.K. the same could be said about fish and chips. In Italy, it's *baccalà* (salt cod). In the case of hamburgers or fish and chips, the recipe never varies much, but the recipe for salt cod changes drastically from region to region in Italy. Don't ask for *baccalà alla Livornese* in Venice or *baccalà mantecato* in Puglia.

It's not hard to imagine why salt cod became the go-to food around the Italian boot. In times before trucks and refrigeration, the transport of fresh fish was impossible. Despite this fact, the Roman Catholic Church mandated days of abstinence when meat could not be eaten. Salted or dried fish became a Friday and Lenten favorite. It had the added benefit of being very inexpensive and was a protein staple for the poor. Cod boasts remarkable nutritional properties: it contains over 18% protein, which once dried rises to almost 80%.

There are two forms of dried codfish—stockfish

and salt cod. Stockfish or *stoccafisso* is made using the smaller cod, dried on sticks in the cold dry air of Scandinavia, creating a very light, easily transported stick fish, thus the name. Salt cod or *baccalà* is created from cod, three to six feet long, split, and salted on wood planks for about ten days, thus only partially drying them. Today, Italy's *baccalà* and *stoccafisso* all come from Norway.

Salt cod has many of the characteristics of fresh cod: large, soft flakes of succulent, opaque flesh with slightly chewy firm texture from the salting, and not at all fishy in flavor. To prepare it, the cook rinses the salt off it and soaks it in cold water for 12 or more hours, depending upon its thickness, changing the water 2-3 times daily. (Stockfish takes a couple of extra days to rehydrate.) Once it has soaked it is skinned, deboned, and ready to be made into the local recipe.

In Veneto, *baccalà* is considered a real delicacy: *Baccalà alla Vicentina* (slowly braised with onions, anchovies and milk) and *Baccalà Mantecato* (a mashed and whipped preparation with extra virgin olive oil, lemon and parsley) are always served with white polenta. Some other popular recipes are *Baccalà alla Livornese* (with tomatoes, garlic, parsley and basil), cooked throughout Tuscany; *Baccalà Fritto* (salt cod chunks fried in a simple egg and flour batter) and *Baccalà all'Agrodolce* (with tomatoes, cooked in wine, flavored with red pepper, pine nuts and sultana raisins), which are both found in Rome. *Baccalà alla Pizzaiola* (salt cod covered with tomatoes, breadcrumbs, capers, plenty of oregano and baked in the oven) and *Baccalà alla Napoletana* (the *baccalà* is fried and then placed in a simmering tomato sauce, with olives, capers and pine nuts) are recipes from Naples. The Neapolitans, even today, boast of the highest consumption of both stockfish and dried salted cod. They claim there are 365 different ways to eat *baccalà*—one for every day of the year.

As you travel around Italy, ask for *baccalà* at least once at each stop to taste the true regionalism of the country.

# DID YOU KNOW?

Salt cod came to the ports of Livorno, Genoa and Naples in the 11th century, brought by Basque sailors, who ventured into the waters of the northern Atlantic, hunting the whales that passed through the Bay of Biscay. They came into contact with the Viking sailors, who dried the fresh-caught cod in the cold dry North Sea winds and then broke it into pieces and chewed it like a biscuit. In the 13th century, the Portuguese, realizing the commercial value of the easily-stored dried fish, cornered the market, sending their ships as far as Greenland. They added salt to dry the fish faster, giving rise to *bacalhau* (derived from the Latin, meaning "*baculus*" or stick). They traded salt cod along the western coast of the Italian peninsula.

The history of baccalà in Venice only dates back to 1431 when a Venetian ship, laden with spices and

800 barrels of Malvasia wine, departed from the island of Crete under the command of the sea captain Piero Querini, and headed for the North Sea and Flanders. When the ship reached the English Channel, the route was disrupted by a violent storm that, after breaking the rudder, blew the ship north for many days. Boarding lifeboats, the crew (only 14 of 68 survived) landed on the uninhabited rock of Sandoy, in Norway's northern Lofoten Islands.

For four months, the Venetians lived with the Norwegian fishermen, and learnt the art of preserving cod. Norway's unique climatic conditions of low temperatures, dry air and a low amount of precipitation were (and still are) perfect for air-drying cod in open tents. Cod preserved in this way can last for years.

Captain Querini returned home with sixty dried stockfish. He told the ruling Doges how the Norwegians dried the fish in the wind until it became as hard and then they beat it and spiced it turning it into a soft and tasty mix. The recipe was known by the Spanish words *baccalà mantecato* (creamed codfish). Querini went back to Norway many times, becoming a major trader in dried and salted codfish.

# DON'T USE BOTTLED ITALIAN
## SALAD DRESSING

To dress a salad in Italy is simplicity itself: bring a bowl of salad greens (preferably one to three varieties of radicchio tossed together–that's all) to the table, add a generous splash of the best extra-virgin olive oil available, a small spray of red-wine vinegar or lemon juice, a substantial sprinkle of salt and a bit of fresh ground black pepper; toss again and serve on a salad plate (don't infect the leafy greens with leftover pasta sauce or juice from the *ossobuco* by re-using those plates).

Note that the ingredients are added to the salad greens sequentially, not shaken into a vinaigrette. The French invented vinaigrette.

Once you master the way to dress an Italian salad, the only debate left is whether inexpensive balsamic vinegar (not the costly traditional DOP ambrosia from Modena) is an acceptable substitute for red-wine vinegar. Purists would say emphatically, "No", but the number of Florentine neighborhood restaurants that bring the sweeter version of vinegar to the table seems to argue for, at least, an acceptable option to the Food Rule.

Italian Dressing, known and loved in the United States (as well as Canada, the U.K. and most of the British colonies), is a vinaigrette-type salad dressing, consisting of water, vinegar or lemon juice, vegetable oil, chopped bell peppers, usually sugar or high fructose corn syrup, and various herbs and spices including oregano, fennel, dill, dried oleoresin paprika and salt. Onion and garlic are often added to intensify the dressing's flavor. Usually it is bought bottled (containing also xanthan gum, calcium disodium edta, and sulfiting agents) or prepared by mixing oil and vinegar with a packaged flavoring mix consisting of dehydrated vegetables and herbs.

North American-style Italian dressing, especially Creamy Italian, which consists of the same ingredients, with buttermilk or mayonnaise added to make it creamy, is not acceptable to the Italian palate. ("*Che schifo*" or "*Che esagerazione!*" say Italians.) Don't ask for it in a restaurant in Italy or, particularly, from the cook in an Italian home.

Italian Dressing is not sold in Italy. Needless to say, you will also not find the following dressings in any Italian kitchen: Thousand Island, Ranch, Blue Cheese, Russian, Louis, Honey Dijon, French, Ginger Honey, and, perhaps surprisingly, Caesar Salad Dressing.

Try being Italian for a while–leave the salad dressing bottles in the fridge and simply add a bit of extra virgin olive oil, red wine vinegar, salt and pepper to some fresh leafy salad greens. You will be surprised by what you taste for the very first time.

# DID YOU KNOW?

Caesar Dressing is much more American than Italian. It is reported that Caesar Cardini created the salad and the dressing in Mexico. Caesar (born Cesare) came from near Lago Maggiore in northern Italy. He and his brother Alex emigrated to the U.S. after World War I. The Cardini family lived in San Diego, but operated a restaurant in Tijuana to circumvent Prohibition. Supposedly, on July 4th in 1924, the salad was created on a busy holiday weekend at Caesar's Restaurant. Caesar was short of supplies, so he concocted this salad with what was on hand: romaine lettuce and croutons dressed with parmesan cheese, lemon juice, olive oil, egg, garlic, black pepper, and Worcestershire sauce. A bit of a showman, he prepared it at the table. This was the only thing truly Italian about Caesar Salad–a salad should be dressed at the table or right before it comes to the table.

# DON'T DIP BISCOTTI IN COFFEE

Italians are very particular about what they dip their biscotti into. Pretty much it is a list of one–Vin Santo.

The subtly sweet, crisp almond cookies are loved throughout the world, but have their origin in Italy. The word "biscotti" is the plural form of *biscotto*, which originates from the ancient Latin word *biscoctus*, meaning "twice-baked." By baking them twice, biscotti (known in Tuscany as *cantucci* or *cantuccini*) lose any excess moisture, which ensures a crisp, dry cookie perfect for dipping. In Vin Santo. Only.

Vin Santo or *vino santo* (holy wine) is a style of Italian dessert wine. Traditional in Tuscany, these sweet high alcohol, late harvest wines are made from white grape varieties such as Trebbiano and Malvasia, which are hung to dry before pressing to increase their sugar content. The most likely origin of the name Vin Santo was the wine's historic use in religious Mass, where sweet wine was often preferred. Some of the earliest references to a *"vinsanto"* wine come from the Renaissance era sales logs of Florentine wine merchants.

So if, after dinner, you start reaching for the biscotti on the plate in the middle of the table to dip into your coffee, stop and think of the number of Italian Food Rules you are about to break—eating after coffee, putting crumbs in coffee, and perhaps, drinking cappuccino after 10am.

First, Italians consider coffee as both a palate cleanser and a *digestivo*. Biscotti and Vin Santo are dessert (*dolce*) and made for each other. Traditional biscotti eaten alone will put your teeth in peril. Dunking them in Vin Santo is the perfect solution. The best sip is the last containing all of the delicious biscotti crumbs.

# THAT'S AMARO – ITALY LOVES IT'S DIGESTIVOS

The smoothly running digestive system is crucial to an Italian's health and happiness. This concern is the basis of so many of the Italian Food Rules. You already know that you do not put uncooked milk on a full stomach (*cappuccino*, *caffellatte*, *gelato*); you do not eat "cold" melon without the "heat" of prosciutto or salt or *peperoncino*; you do not eat leftovers; and you do not overeat. Having eaten *well*, however, an Italian may partake of an herbal digestive drink after dinner.

The first attempts to aid digestion using aromatic herbs and seeds steeped in liquids were made by the Greeks and Romans. Yet today, no country can match Italy for the sheer variety of digestive remedies available. They traveled from the pharmacies of the 1800s, intended as palliatives to counter all sorts of ailments and physical imbalances, to restaurants, bars and the dinner table in the 20th century. They are bitter–that's *amaro*.

These homemade restoratives, generally bitter

herbs, plants and other botanicals blended into an alcohol base, live on commercially today in the form of digestives. Digestives are not the usual after-dinner drinks, like brandies, grappas and other distilled products that are meant to add a pleasant intoxicating after-note to a meal, or the sweet high-alcohol wines, like Vin Santo, which give you a final sweet taste, but not the fullness of a three-layer cake.

These digestives, or *digestivi*, are known collectively as *amari*. The word refers to the bitterness that unifies this disparate group of liqueurs. Dozens of *amari* are produced in Italy. Each has a proprietary formula made by distilling a wide variety of herbs and spices and tempered in barrels or bottles. *Amari* have been toted in Italy to cure overeating, flatulence, hangovers, gas pains, cramps of all kinds, baby colic and cholera. One theory is that bitterness, typically associated with poison, cues the body to accelerate the production of saliva and digestive juices.

No one *amaro* shares the same makeup or ingredients with another. For example: Amaro Averna from Sicily is comprised of citrus, herbs, roots, and caramel; Cynar is an *amaro* made from 13 herbs and artichokes (*Cynara scolymus*), from which the drink derives its name; Nocino, is a *digestivo* made from green walnuts; Unicum, formerly a Hungarian *amaro*, contains 40 herbs and is aged in oak casks (the Zwak family, holder of the secret Unicum recipe, emigrated to Italy after WWII); Vecchio Amaro del Capo, a herbal and minty *amaro* is made in Calabria; and Fernet-Branca, probably the most world-famous *amaro*, is made from a secret recipe of 27 herbs obtained from five continents.

Don't succumb to the distasteful practice of doing Fernet-Branca shots at your local bar in Los Angeles or New York in an effort to be cool. Sip a small glass after a four-course dinner at you favorite restaurant in Turin or Milan.

## DID YOU KNOW?

Fernet-Branca was created by a self-taught herbalist in Milan in 1845. The secret recipe for this *digestivo*, first sold in pharmacies, includes aloe from South Africa, rhubarb from China, gentian from France, galangal from India or Sri Lanka, chamomile from Italy and Argentina, saffron, red cinchona bark, myrrh from Madagascar (yes, that's right–myrrh), and elderflower. The brew is aged in oak barrels for twelve months. It is about 40% alcohol. Fernet Branca is considered by some as a perfect cure for a hangover, but Italians drink it as a *digestivo* after a long meal.

Nocino is an *amaro* that can be found in most restaurants and ordered as a *digestivo*. But it is also the most popular *amaro* for the home-made *digestivo*, probably because of the ease of its recipe. Its main ingredient is green walnuts picked long before they are ready to eat.

The regions of Campania and Emilia-Romagna are the biggest producer of walnuts in Italy. Traditionally, the walnuts are picked by a woman (there is a bit of the pagan about this concoction) on the eve of June 24th, the *Festa di San Giovanni* (St. John the Baptist's saint day), the recipe is made the next day, after the *noci* have rested overnight, and then the brew is put away until *Ognissanti* (All Saints Day), November 1st, when it is drunk to honor the dead. Thereafter, it is sipped as a *digestivo* after the big December holiday meals.

To make Nocino, the walnuts (*noci*) are cleaned and quartered, put into round glass bottles with a mixture of alcohol, sugar, cinnamon, and cloves and allowed to rest in a warm sunny place. The liquid seeps into the nuts and turns dark brown. More sugar and spices are added and, if the liquid has become too strong, a little water is added.

Pellegrino Artusi (1820-1911), the father of modern Italian cooking, reportedly suffered from a "delicate stomach" and noted in his seminal cookbook that the digestive and tonic powers of this dark and sweet liqueur were the perfect end to those heavier meals later on in the year when the cooler months arrive. Artusi's Nocino contained unripe walnuts, alcohol (95%), white sugar, ground cinnamon, whole cloves, water, and the rind of one lemon. Sealed tightly in a large glass vessel, stored in a warm place, shaken "every now and then", the concoction was ready in forty days or so. A couple of days before November 1st he would have a little taste. If it was too "*spiritoso*" (too high in alcohol), Artusi advised adding a cup of water or two. Then, when the liqueur is ready, strain it first through a cloth, and then to clarify it, again through a finer cloth or paper, such as a modern coffee filter, before bottling.

Artusi also recommended an *amaro* he called "Cinchona Elixir" made with "bruised Peruvian cinchona bark" and "bruised dried bitter orange peel."

# DON'T ASK FOR A DOGGY BAG

The Italian Food Rule: Don't Ask for a Doggy Bag, has strange antecedents because, according to some, the doggy bag's first appearance was in the 6th century BC...in Rome. Apparently, when invited to a banquet at the neighbor's villa the ancient Roman would bring a napkin or two. It was a compliment to the host to take some of the dinner home wrapped up in your napkin. But perhaps with the fall of the empire the custom fell into disfavor. During the Middle Ages, the leftovers went first to the kitchen staff, then to the lower order of servants, and then out the backdoor to the beggars in the courtyard.

In modern times, there seem to be three reasons that Italians don't ask for a take-out container. (The term doggy bag or doggie bag is an Americanism that entered the European lexicon mostly to complain about the practice.)

First, Italian food is made to order, to be eaten as the chef envisioned it, immediately as the dish arrives on the table. It is not to be eaten at another temperature (cold pizza), in another form (*bistecca alla fiorentina* sliced in a sandwich), or mixed together (*pasta alla carbonara* with a chunk off a veal chop resting on top).

Second, servings in Italian restaurants tend to be of the appropriate size so that the diner does not get too full by eating everything on the plate. A light eater does not order an *antipasto*, a *primo*, a *secondo*, and a *dolce*—one or two courses are enough.

Third, Italians look at food left on the plate as scraps, not leftovers. There's a difference. It's not good manners to ask to take home kitchen scraps.

I learned about this Italian Food Rule years ago, when I was a regular at La Maremma on Via Verdi in Florence. One evening, I ordered my favorite pasta and then saw ostrich (*filetto di struzzo con salsa di vino rosso*) on the menu. The owner, Enzo Ragazzini, explained that the ostrich was grown in Italy and urged me to try "*un piatto speciale e buono.*" I agreed, forgetting to ask for a half-portion of the pasta. After some shared *crostini*, my large plate of *penne con funghi e tartufi* arrived, steaming, fragrant, and oh so scrumptious. I just had to eat the whole thing.

Almost full, my eyes popped wide when a beautifully presented filet of ostrich—round, about two inches high and four inches in diameter, like a classic filet mignon at a good steakhouse in the U.S.—with a deep purple-brown wine sauce and a sprig of fresh rosemary, was placed in front of me.

The *filetto* was perfect, pink, tender, complemented in every way by the accompanying sauce. But it was huge. I could not do it justice in one sitting.

Not after that pasta (and *crostini* and wine). I could have shared it with my friends, but as luck would have it I was eating with two vegetarians.

I couldn't let half a filet of ostrich, my first ostrich dish, go to waste. And I did not want the chef to get the wrong idea–I loved every bite. So I asked Enzo in my almost non-existent Italian, if there was any way he could wrap the half filet up so I could take it back to my apartment. This conversation took a while. He even resorted to some English to clarify my desire. After I finally came up with "*da portare via, per favore,*" a phrase more suited to a pastry shop than a restaurant, he left with the plate, shaking his head.

He returned in a bit and showed me a small used, but clean, plastic bag with a warm aluminum-wrapped half filet of ostrich. I reach for it to put it quickly in my shopping satchel, out of sight. He wouldn't let it go. He sat down at the table and in a mix of Italian and English proceeded to give me the recipe (did I mention that I do not cook?) for the red wine sauce that graced the filet on the original plate. He could not envision it being served any other way.

He could not imagine that I would slice this tender filet of ostrich up with a little mustard and mayo in a *panino*, or toss it into a microwave oven to warm it up to go on a plate beside a similarly zapped potato (my kind of cooking). No, I was instructed on how to make the exact same wine sauce as the chef. I took notes.

# DID YOU KNOW?

In Rome the Italian Food Rule: Don't Ask for a Doggy Bag is starting to crumble. Some say that Michelle Obama is to blame. In 2009, Michelle was in Rome during the G8 Conference. Michelle, together with her two daughters, dined at a restaurant near the Pantheon. The family ordered three pasta dishes—*carbonara*, *amatriciana* and *bolognese*—but the meal turned out to be too hearty for the three Obama girls. Michelle asked the waiter to pack the leftovers into a bag to take home. According to the news reports, the First Lady's effort to make sure the food did not go to waste was widely understood as a public encouragement to save more and waste less.

By 2010, a non-profit group that works with homeless people in Milan, *Cena dell'Amicizia*, began a project called "*Il buono che avanza*," ("the good that advances" or "the good things left over"). Restaurants in the Milan area can voluntarily take part, whereupon they are provided with doggy bags and an "*Il buono che avanza*" sticker created by the non-profit organization. "The idea is to fight the idea of a throw-away, consumerist society where waste is normal and recycling (even of food) is looked down upon," claimed *Cena dell'Amicizia*.

From all appearances, Florence, Tuscany and most of the rest of Italy will hold tight to the Italian Food Rule: Don't Ask for a Doggy Bag. Leftovers do not constitute food in a country that prides itself in a cuisine that has not seen change in centuries and is not ready for reheating in the modern microwave oven.

# TAKE-AWAY PIZZA RULES

Before the turn of the millennium, pizza delivery was rare. In fact, prepared food delivery is almost unheard of in Italy because food is meant to be eaten hot, not tepid and not reheated, with fresh ingredients, tasting exactly as the cook envisioned the dish. This is especially important for pizza, which now can be delivered in most mid-sized to large cities by a guy on a Vespa, or picked up at the corner pizzeria and taken back to your hotel room.

Eating pizza in Italy is supposed to be a social event to be enjoyed with friends in a festive setting. Not on the kitchen table, half-warm, out of a cardboard box.

Pizza is never, never, never to be eaten as a leftover, cold or nuked, while standing in your kitchen.

Pizza made by a *pizzaiolo* in a wood-burning pizza oven (the only pizza worth eating) is a delicate thing. The crust is thin, the sauce is fine and fresh, and the other ingredients are newly sliced and few. Within minutes after it is slid via a special paddle (the loading peel) from the fiery maw of the oven, it must be eaten immediately or it will be only a figment of its former gloriousness.

Leftover pizza is table scrap—literally, it is meant to be thrown away in the nearest bin—not to be put in a box, congealed mozzarella and mushroom bits, and all, to be carried home or to your hotel minibar fridge.

Treat pizza with the respect it (and the *pizzaiolo*) deserves and eat it hot and fast in a noisy pizzeria with friends. It's worth that first-bite blister on your palate. Better that you remember that pain the next day, rather than noshing on the soggy remnants of a once savory slice.

# KISS THAT PANINO

Keep It Simple Stupid (KISS) is what an Italian would say looking at the sandwiches Americans love to eat. Now that "*panini*" are all the rage in the U.S. makes the overloaded sandwiches all the more egregious. A *panino* is *pane* (bread) with an *–ino* suffix to denote a small roll. Inside the small roll (not sliced bread) should be one or two slices of one or two, possibly three, ingredients. The idea is to be able to *taste* each ingredient, not to have them become some indecipherable jumble of flavors.

A foot-long sandwich with ten different spreads, cheeses, meats and lettuces is not Italian. The term *panino* as used in the U.S. usually means a sandwich that is heated under a *panino* press. The machine might have been invented in Italy, but not all *panini* are heated. Most are not because, again, the idea is to taste each ingredient. Also, butter never enters the equation–you will never find a buttered, toasted sandwich in Italy.

Venice is famed for its sliced bread (without a

crust) enclosing one to three ingredients and mayonnaise (mayo is not found in *panini* in other regions).
These are not *panini*, but are Venetian *tramezzini*,
which like all other regional specialties, should only
be eaten in Venice, where they know how to make
them.

If you see large sandwiches in glassed cases of
coffee bars and self-serve eateries in the popular
tourist towns of Florence, Rome and Venice, be
aware that they are probably stale, are not traditional
*panini* and are eaten only by foreigners. If you see
Italians lining up at a window of a tiny shop where
small warm, soft rolls of white bread are being torn
open and filled with a thin slice of folded *mortadella*
(no mayonnaise or mustard) or perhaps, a smear of
goat cheese and a couple of slices of a spicy *salame*,
get in line and have the best *panino* of your life.

# DON'T EAT WHILE WALKING

Italians never eat or drink while they're walking. They have no culture of snacking on the types of food that Americans are frequently noshing on as they hurry from place to place–no Big Gulps, bags of Cool Ranch Doritos, Big Macs, or even, a *panino con la mortadella* (bologna sandwich). (Yes, sadly there are Big Macs in Italy, but they are being eaten–slowly–while at the table provided, not on the run.) There are no take-away sippy cups for coffee or cappuccino in Italy.

This aversion to eating and drinking while walking is learned at a young age. It's taught by a mother who values spotless clothes on her offspring and wants her family at the table on time and hungry, not stuffed with chips or a giant soda before the meal even begins. Italians stay thin by eating three meals a day at a table, not grazing on their feet, on the run.

So what about *gelato*? Yes, it is an exception to the rule. Italians walk while licking a small (2.50 € or less) cone–a cone, not a cup–of *gelato*. If you are eating gelato out of a cup, you should be sitting in the *gelateria* or on a nearby bench. If you order a large cone (more than 2 scoops) you are not Italian.

While Americans are eating on the run to the next meeting, the Italians are sitting at a table, taking small mouthfuls, resting their cutlery between bites, discussing the food—because it is worthy of discussion. In case you were wondering, Italians do not eat in the car, either.

# ITALIANS DON'T SNACK

There are Pringles, corn chips, candy, chewing gum, Cokes (not Pepsi), canned sweetened ice tea, Tic-Tacs, M&Ms and Mars Bars in any coffee bar or small grocery store in Italy. But who buys these snacks? Tourists…mostly.

Traditionally, Italians don't snack…with a couple of exceptions. First, at around 11am, Italians will stop by the local bar for an espresso. Between 4pm and 6pm and between 11pm and midnight, they will visit the gelateria for a small (maximum two scoops) cone. In the winter, the afternoon espresso may be changed out for a hot chocolate (*cioccolato caldo*) and the gelato may be forsaken for a hot fresh-made *bombolone* (fried doughnut). Also, in the winter a small bag of hot roasted chestnuts may become an early evening snack before dinner.

The name for these snacks is *merenda*, derived from the Latin "*mereo*", which means "that which you should deserve"–a well-deserved snack.

In Venice, the afternoon *merenda* is sometimes known as *l'ombra*. It consists of a small glass of wine and a bite or two of *cicheti* (tapas-like salty offerings, perhaps anchovies, olives, or tiny fried fish). *Cicheti* comes from the Latin *"ciccus"* (small quantity). The term *ombra* means shade. Supposedly, long ago purveyors of wine moved their carts around the *piazza* to keep their wine cool in the shade.

The world has long wondered why the pasta-eating Italians don't get fat. The answers are portion control and no snacking in between meals. Since Italians don't eat while walking (another Food Rule) the consumption of snacks is naturally controlled to a large extent. Italian mothers do the rest.

Some will say that the snack prohibition is a thing of the past and sadly they are correct. With both mothers and fathers at work, latchkey kids are enjoying fast food lunches (a.k.a. snacks) and illicit snacks at any time in the afternoon. Although you will rarely see an Italian child walking with a can of Coke in his hand, the frequent sight of chubby children tells a story of its own.

## DID YOU KNOW?

Italians denote small things by adding the singular *-ina* or *-ino* or the plural *–ine* or *–ini* on to the end of the word. A tiny snack would therefore become *merendina*. Italian expert on food and culture, Massimo Montanari, postulates that the more frequent use of the diminutive *merendina* has the effect of "de-ritualizing" the two daily breaks for "well-deserved refreshment" and creating a culture of tiny snacks or snacking that by its very nature can be done at any time, instead of the traditional times for *merenda*. So those candy bars at the cash register of every coffee bar are possibly becoming less for tourists and more for those Italians with ever-expanding waistlines.

# ITALIANS DON'T SNACK - THEY EAT NUTELLA

Italians stay thin (at least, in the near past), because they follow two of the Italian Food Rules: 1) No Eating While Walking; and 2) No Snacking. But then there is Nutella.

Nutella (for those who live in another universe) is a creamy chocolate-hazelnut confection that spreads like peanut butter (a food that hasn't ever gained a foothold in the Italian cupboard). The Ferrero chocolate company created Nutella as a special *merenda* (an afternoon refreshment) for children to replace the milk- or water- or wine-soaked slice of bread sprinkled with sugar that was offered up by most mothers prior to 1950. Nutella was marketed as a healthy alternative because of the protein from the hazelnuts.

Nutella only made an appearance as an after-school snack because during World War II in Italy there was an exorbitant tax on rare cocoa beans that almost destroyed the Italian chocolate industry. In 1944, Ferrero (then a bakery in the Piemonte region where hazelnuts were plentiful) created a chocolate-like mixture made of 71.5% hazelnut paste and 19.5% chocolate. At first it was marketed as *gianduia*, a tiny wrapped morsel. But children tended to throw the bread away and just eat the candy. Ferrero remade the concoction as a spread in a small jar.

After the war ended and chocolate was still expensive and in short supply, Ferrero's *Supercrema* was the most popular chocolate substitute. Children would go to the local store with a slice of bread in hand for a smear of Ferrero's spread, costing 5 lire (less than a penny). These children were hooked and Nutella (the name came in 1963, emphasizing the nut, not the chocolate) became part of the Italian food culture.

Today, the main ingredients of Nutella are sugar and palm oil, followed by hazelnut, cocoa solids and skimmed milk. Italians will still argue that eating Nutella is not "snacking" because it is only eaten on bread as a *merenda* at 4pm…or in crepes at the beach…or for a special filling for a weekend breakfast pastry…or on a spoon, whenever.

## DID YOU KNOW?

In the United States, a New Jersey mother and a California mother took Ferrero USA to court in February 2011, in two separate cases, claiming that Nutella was deceptively marketed, advertised, and sold in the United States as a "healthy" and "nutritious" food. The court documents claimed Nutella's marketing and advertising was misleading because it claimed that "Nutella is a "wholesome" food product and can be served as part of a "balanced" and "nutritious breakfast," but "omits that the nutritional value claimed, if any, is not derived from Nutella, but is instead derived from other foods or drinks (e.g., whole grain breads, fruit and milk), which are advertised to be consumed along with Nutella." They went on to say that Nutella's marketing claims were false and misleading because "they omit that Nutella contains high levels of saturated fat, the consumption of which has been shown to increase the blood cholesterol levels" and "they omit that Nutella contains over 55% processed sugar, the consumption of which has been shown to cause type 2 diabetes and other serious health problems."

In September 2012, it was announced that Ferrero USA had settled with the class action claimants for just over $3 million (estimated payout to claimants, now numbering in the thousands, is $4 to $20).

A lawsuit against Nutella would never happen in Italy.

# No All-You-Can-Eat Buffets

If you come across an all-you-can-eat-buffet in Italy, you have made a rare sighting and are probably at a tourist trap (bad food) or a hotel restaurant (not necessarily bad food, but not served in an Italian manner). An all-you-can-eat-buffet breaks the following Italian Food Rules: 1) Menu Rules (separate plates for each dish, served in a specified order), 2) Pasta is Not a Side Dish, 3) No Eating Bread with Pasta, and 4) Don't Pass the Gravy (a variant in this case–don't mix the sauces).

Italians don't quite know how to act when faced with a buffet table loaded with foods that are usually regarded as appetizers, first dishes (pasta or risotto), or entrées, along with a bunch of side dishes. First, they are not sure if they should select only one food, return to their seats and eat it, thus following the rules that govern the mixing of flavors on one plate. Second, they don't know whether it is proper to eat pasta before an appetizer. Third, they don't know when bread should come into play in the meal. And finally, Italians aren't sure that the platters are going to be refilled, so they tend to rush the table.

There is an "Italian" food chain in the U.S. that serves a dish called "Tour of Italy" that is a plate of "Homemade Lasagna, Lightly Breaded Chicken Parmigiana, and Creamy Fettuccine Alfredo." It adds up to 1,450 calories, 33 grams of saturated fat, and 3,830 milligrams of sodium. It is an all-you-can-eat buffet on a plate. And it breaks all of the above-mentioned Italian Food Rules and a couple more: 1) Alfredo is a name, not a pasta sauce, and 2) no Parmesan cheese on breaded chicken.

American Thanksgiving in Italy creates a similar situation to a loaded buffet table. In late November, Americans start searching for a whole turkey to roast (hard to find in any Italian market because the butcher usually cuts up the large fowl into easy to cook pieces—a stuffed, roast turkey is not an Italian dish). Whether the bird is found or not, the invitations go out. The Americans on the guest list all bring a side dish, perhaps a traditional Thanksgiving recipe or an Italian one. The Italians bring wine, chocolates or flowers. There is too much food for the normal table so another is set up nearby. Now it becomes a Thanksgiving buffet.

I remember my first Thanksgiving in Italy. The guest list contained eight Americans and two Italians. One of the Italians had experienced Thanksgiving in the U.S. and knew the drill. The other was a retired executive of a famous Italian luxury brand and though he had lived in New York for years, he had never before experienced Thanksgiving dinner. As could be expected, the Americans descended on the buffet table (in this case, the island in the open kitchen) with gusto, loading our plates with a slice of turkey, chestnut and mushroom stuffing, mashed potatoes, Parmesan creamed spinach, a couple of liver pâté *crostini*, some rare cranberry sauce, small polenta muffins, dinner rolls and turkey gravy poured over the potatoes and meat.

The Italian Thanksgiving aficionado scooped small portions of what she would consider to be appetizers from two or three platters, carefully segregating them to different areas on her plate. She sat down and finished each completely, before she went back to get small servings of turkey, mashed potatoes and stuffing. The retired Italian executive–a Thanksgiving newbie–looked in horror at the heaped plates of the Americans, took a couple of crostini and sat down. He ate them and went back to get turkey and mashed potatoes, but no gravy. He finished that, cleaned his plate with small piece of a dinner roll and went back for a taste of stuffing and some green beans. This was a man, like most Italians, who would never consider dining at an all-you-can-eat buffet.

# WHAT GOES TOGETHER –
## TOMATO, MOZZARELLA, & BASIL

Probably the most famous food or ingredient pairing in Italy is that of fresh tomato, mozzarella cheese, and fresh basil. More than any other country, Italy prides itself in being able to pair not only wine with food, but also ingredient to ingredient–food to food.

Fresh, creamy, barely salty, mozzarella cuts the acid/sweet taste of sliced vine-ripened tomatoes. Add a sprig of fresh basil to provide an accent and you have the perfect dish, known throughout the world as *Caprese*. All that is needed is a splash of extra virgin olive oil and a bit of salt and fresh cracked black pepper.

In texture this combination is also compatible as the soft mushiness of the cheese vies with the crisp crunch of the tomato.

There can be no compromise on the pairing of ingredients in *Caprese*. Salty hard aged parmesan cannot be substituted for fresh mozzarella. Bland zucchini can't take the place of ripe tomatoes. In fact, the somewhat green, watery, traveled-a-thousand-miles tomatoes found in the U.S., or canned tomatoes, or even peeled tomatoes, cannot take the place of a mature sweet, vine-ripened, small- to medium-sized tomato. Oregano or thyme or rosemary or any other herb—even dried basil—cannot be substituted for fresh green leaves of basil, preferably growing in a pot on your windowsill.

Finally, the look of *Caprese* is quintessential Italy. *Tri-colore*—red, white and green—the colors of the Italian flag.

# WHAT GOES TOGETHER –
## PROSCIUTTO & MELON

The second most famous Italian food pairing is prosciutto and melon. Prosciutto, pink, salty and dry, is the perfect wrap for the orange, sweet, juicy cantaloupe.

Serve the melon peeled and sliced in long crescents with one slice of prosciutto wrapped around each piece to be eaten with a knife and fork. Or wrap a small cube or ball of melon in a tiny sack of prosciutto for perfect finger food.

The melon must be in season and as sweet as can be. Prosciutto is always available and it is a matter of taste whether the famous Prosciutto di Parma is selected or the saltier Tuscan variety from the *Cinta Sinese* pork is desired.

As with all Italian ingredient pairings, no substitutes will do. Don't wrap a slice of baked Virginia ham or of roasted *prosciutto di Praga* around a spear of watermelon or a piece of green honeydew melon. The taste will be wrong. The texture will be wrong, and the color combination will not delight the Italian eye.

# DID YOU KNOW?

Eating melons without the prosciutto is considered somewhat dangerous to Italians. It comes down to an issue of digestion, as many things do in regard to the Italian Food Rules. If a "cold" food, like melon, is eaten without a "hot" balancing food, like a salty meat or spicy chili peppers, the body is "chilled", which leads to the dreaded *congestione*, or at least, indigestion.

There is historical proof for this claim. In July 1471, Pope Paul II died after a dinner consisting of three cantaloupes. The melons were to blame. In 1602, Giacomo della Porta, the architect of another pope, died after reportedly eating too much cantaloupe and watermelon, causing fatal indigestion when his organs became chilled.

# WHAT GOES TOGETHER –
## SALAME & FIGS

Salty and sweet of the highest degree meet in the pairing of figs with *salame*. This is the perfect snack or *antipasto*. It's a finger food–either roll up the juicy fig in a thin slice of *salame* and pop it in your mouth or, if the in-laws are invited, you may wish to pre-wrap the figs, skewer with a toothpick, and avoid any hand to mouth ineptness.

Don't get fancy here in your selection of *salame*. A simple cured variety large enough to wrap a fig is all you need. Avoid truffled salame or a wine infused variety. If you want to be a bit bold, try *salame di cinghiale*–wild boar *salame*.

It must be *salame*. Prosciutto is too bland. Baked ham is just wrong.

Rachael Ray promotes a recipe with cooked "salami and fig preserves". That's American, not Italian. Italians do not heat up their fabulous hand made, long-cured, perfect-as-they-are *salami*, except if they are adding *salame piccante* to a *pizza diavola*, but only then and there isn't going to be a fig in sight.

Wait for fresh fig season. Italians don't settle for fig preserves. Many Italians will skin the fig, but it is not strictly necessary if they've been given a good wash or if you are lucky enough to have your own fig tree and a convenient *salame* and a sharp knife.

## DID YOU KNOW?

The word "salami" used by English-speakers, is the plural form of the Italian word "*salame*". In English it does not matter if there are one or two encased, cured meats or a bunch of slices ready to be wrapped around figs, it's still salami. In Italy, it matters: If you want two long uncut encased, cured meats hanging from the butcher's ceiling, you ask for "*due salami*". If you want about ten thin slices to go around your ten small figs, ask for "*un etto di salame*" (100 grams of *salame*).

# WHAT GOES TOGETHER – FRESH FAVA BEANS & PECORINO

Hannibal Lecter made fava beans famous, but his food pairing was, to say the least…wrong. Most people think of fava beans as a banal dried legume that takes hours to cook or the forgettable part of a soup or stew. The ideal pairing of fava beans (sometimes called "broad beans") is when they are fresh and eaten with pecorino cheese.

Fresh fava beans do not have the same following in the world as they do in Italy, probably because the season is so short. Tuscans call these fava beans "*baccelli*". They are at their best only in the spring, when the pods are relatively short and the beans are small and tender. Left too long on the vine the beans grow a tough skin and they must be cooked or dried to be eatable.

Italians like to eat the slightly bitter bean with small slices of a barely-aged, but flavorful, sheep's milk cheese, called *Marzolino*, the pecorino only made in the month of March when the flocks have access to the sweetest grasses and most tender herbs.

The light green *baccelli* with their slightly sharp taste and crunchy texture make a perfect match to creamy slightly salty aromatic cheese. Sometimes the beans are left in their pods and placed in the center of the Italian table on a large platter with the small wheel of pecorino *Marzolino* on a cutting board beside it. In this manner it is a finger-food appetizer where all of the diners get to hull their own beans and slice the cheese to accompany the *baccelli*.

More commonly, the shelling happens in the kitchen where the cook cubes the cheese to about the same size as the hulled beans, and then tosses them together in a bowl with a splash of olive oil, a shake of sea salt and plenty of coarsely ground fresh black pepper. The dish is then served as an antipasto.

Next time you are in Italy in the spring, go to the closest vegetable vendor and buy a kilo of *baccelli*. Then, stop by the *latteria* and pick up a half kilo of *Marzolino*. All you need after that is a knife before you will be able to taste one of the best food pairings Italy has to offer.

## DID YOU KNOW?

Historically, shepherds made *Marzolino* cheese from the season's first sheep's milk obtained when the flocks were able to go back to the pasture after the winter. *Marzolino* is the youngest of the pecorino cheeses, with a soft light skin (sometimes pale orange in color), shaped in an oval form, weighing about one pound. It has a micro-season and is only supposed to be eaten in March as the name indicates. The taste of the cheese reflects the season's first grasses and herbs eaten by the ewes. The curds are wrapped in the leaves of the cardoon, further infusing it with its famous spicy grassy flavor. *Marzolino*, was perfected in Tuscany, enjoyed by the Medici Grand Dukes, taken to Rome by Michelangelo, and two centuries earlier, immortalized by Boccaccio in the *Decameron*.

# WHAT GOES TOGETHER – PEAR & PECORINO

There is an ancient Italian saying from the days when the farming system was such that 50% of the farmer's crop went to the landowner and 10% went to the church–*al contadino non far sapere quant'è buono il cacio con le pere*–don't tell the farmer how good cheese tastes with pears. Since the farmer milked the ewes, made the cheese and picked the pears, the landowners and priests had a right to fear their portions would be shorted.

One of the world's leading experts on food and culture, Massimo Montanari, wrote a 128-page book, entitled *Il Formaggio con le Pere: La Storia in un Proverbio* (Cheese with Pears: The History in a Proverb), which unravels the origin and use throughout history of the saying.

The right cheese with the right fruit is the key to Italian food pairing. The proper cheese is an aged *pecorino*, made from sheep's milk, salty with a stronger flavor than cow's milk cheese. (There are some Italians who argue for a younger creamier cheese, but they still agree that it must be *pecorino*.)

The pears must be mature, but crisp–sweet, but not mushy. Some claim Bartlett pears are best, but no one puts up much of an argument, unless you try to substitute another fruit.

This is a white on white dish because Italians *always* peel their fruit before eating it. The dish can be presented as pear crescents alternated with thin slices of *pecorino* or the pears can be halved and the *pecorino* shaved (not grated) in curls on top of the fruit or finally the pear and cheese can be cut in equal sized cubes and tossed together. One daring chef tried to solve the problem of over-ripe pears by creating a fruit sauce to spread on cheese. Try this for your Italian friends at your peril.

# DON'T TOUCH THE FRUITS AND VEGETABLES

Food shoppers in the U.S. feel free to poke, prod, squeeze, thump and sniff the fruits and vegetables whether they plan to buy the produce or not. At a *fruttivendolo* stand in Italy that habit will garner you a withering look and a command to unhand the eggplant: "*Non tocchi le melanzane, per favore!*"

One of the pleasures of life in Italy is the taste of vine-ripened (or tree-ripened) fruits and vegetables. This is a major reason Italian food is so good–there are fresh local ingredients at the perfect level of ripeness. They are a feast for eye as well as the stomach. This also makes the produce delicate to the touch, even if you don't have the outsized fear of germs that most Italians have.

The Italian Food Rule: Don't Touch the Fruits and Vegetables, has its basis in both the protection of the produce and the desire to reduce the spread of disease.

The proper procedure is to approach a shopkeeper and say *"buongiorno"* followed by saying exactly what you'd like to buy. You'll have to deal with weights and/or numbers. *"Un chilo di fagiolini, per favore"*–a kilo (2.2 pounds) of green beans, please; *"Tre cipolle, per favore"*–three onions, please; or harder still for the metrically-challenged: *"Quattro etti di zucchine, per favore"*–four hectograms (400 grams) of zucchini.

It's considered rude to tell the *fruttivendola* exactly which fruit she should put in your bag. She's the expert. Locals will tell a vendor when they plan to eat their fruit and she'll use her expertise to pick those at the appropriate stage of ripeness, especially for the repeat customers she wants to keep happy. If you want ripe fruit to eat today, add clarification, *"da mangiare oggi, per favore"*–to eat today, please.

Sometimes a vendor will tell you to just go ahead and pick out your own fruit, or you can request permission by asking, *"Posso?"* (May I?). Then wait for a nod or the passing of a plastic or paper sack for your use. But just because you have permission to select your own potatoes, doesn't mean they want to see you rooting through the bin tossing your rejects hither and yon. You're expected to carefully select and touch only those items you wish to buy, unless there's obviously something wrong with them. It's all about hygiene.

You may have the luck to find the one or two produce vendors in Italy who love foreigners and take pride in providing all of their customers, new and old, with the very best fruit and vegetables they have to offer. Do not feel bad if this is not the case on the day you are shopping for figs and plums. The *ortolano* may not have your best interests at heart. It most likely has less to do with the fact that you don't speak Italian with the local accent as it has to do with the fact that you are not a regular customer and he has produce he needs to offload.

One of my most memorable experiences when I followed this Italian Food Rule to my regret came on the day I wanted to buy three large fresh porcini mushrooms. I went to a stand in Florence's *Mercato Centrale* where the vendor only sold mushrooms–the expert. There was even an example of his high quality porcini split in half exposing its firm white worm-free center.

I followed the Italian Food Rule: Don't Touch the Produce. I asked for three large porcini with stems and caps. He selected three fine looking specimens and placed them carefully in a paper bag. I trudged home with my sacks of shopping, unloaded them on the table and discovered that one of my fine mushrooms had a toothpick holding the cap to the stem and was turning slightly brown at the center. But there were no worms.

Buying groceries at an Italian supermarket is easier. You get to touch the produce, but not with your bare hands. At Coop or Esselunga or Conad, it won't be the vendor upholding the Italian Food Rule: Don't Touch the Fruits and Vegetables. It will be Italian housewives, young to very old, enforcing a subset of the Rule: Don't touch the produce without a plas-

tic glove. A withering look from an Italian grandmother is just scary. A sarcastic comment is even
more frightening.

One of the pleasures of living in Italy is shopping at the food markets. The produce is fresher and
more flavorful than at the supermarket. Find an *orto-
lana* who treats you right and then get to know her,
asking her advice about what to buy and how to cook
it, greeting her even when not shopping for produce.
It is a relationship that can last, seemingly, a lifetime
and can save you from finding a toothpick in your
porcini.

## Did You Know?

You'll find plastic gloves near the plastic bags in
the section with the fruits and vegetables, and you're
expected to use them. This is the procedure for buying loose vegetables and fruits in a supermarket:

1) Find a plastic glove; 2) Put it on; 3) Get a
plastic bag for each of your desired fruits or vegetables; 4) Select your produce from the bins; 5) Look
for and remember the code on the bin's label; 6)
Place your bag on the nearby scale and push the button that corresponds to the code; and 7) Wait for a
printed sticker to exit the scale and paste it on outside of the bag.

If you don't follow this procedure, the checker
will have to do it for you when you check out (or
worse, will send you back to do it), much to the dis-
pleasure of the people in the line behind you.

# ITALIANS EAT LOCAL AND IN SEASON

Italians eat food made from ingredients that are seasonal and produced locally. This is the basis for the quality of Italian food in Italy.

That is not to say the food is the same throughout the peninsula. The reason that there are so many discussions taking place in Italy among Italians about which region has the best bread or wine or fish or pasta sauce or *ravioli* or cheese or *bistecca* or extra virgin olive oil, is that each region produces its own ingredients locally and the recipes have been passed down for centuries. But the quality of the ingredients is uniformly superior throughout the country because Italians eat in season and use local ingredients.

Yes, fruit from South America arrives during the winter in Italy, but, by and large, the Italians don't buy the imports because their mothers have told them that you only eat citrus in the winter, apples in the fall, and strawberries in the summer.

Tomatoes do not travel thousands of miles to Italian markets, arriving partially green and tasteless.

Each type of tomato, the one selected as perfect for the recipe, arrives in season, vine-ripened and sweet (except for those specifically left slightly green for salads and those picked very early for a Tuscan fried green tomato *frittata*).

As you travel throughout Italy, do not try to order a dish that is the specialty of Venice in Rome or a recipe from Rome in a Florentine trattoria. Ask a local where to eat and what to eat. Drink the local wine—it will complement the local food. While in Italy, join the Italians in eating food made of ingredients that are in season and produced locally.

# ITALIAN

## *Life*

### RULES

# BY WAY OF INTRODUCTION

In 1998, I quit my job at a law firm in San Francisco and went off to Italy, on not much more than a whim, for nine months. Maybe it was a severe case of job burnout, but I blithely thought the experience was going to be a personalized version of a two-semester graduate school course without the trips home for winter and spring breaks. I called it a Master of Arts in Italy with a major in art, history and language and a minor in food and wine. I knew virtually nothing about Italy, except for vague memories of a week in 1977 when I traveled the length of the peninsula with two Canadians I barely knew in their secondhand Citroën.

This time I came with a plan. Having signed up for three months of classes at the *Centro di Cultura per Stranieri dell'Università di Firenze*, I would study Beginning Italian every morning for four hours. I rented an apartment in Borgo degli Albizi not far from the Duomo in the historic center. A novice in the kitchen I took cooking classes from the "Diva", Judy Witts, at her school Divina Cucina. I studied Dante's Inferno and Early Renaissance Art at the British Institute of Florence. I rented a car and toured the Chianti Classico region, with an idea of learning about Italian wine, but found myself more interested in the history of World War II and the course of battles in Tuscany after finding the strangely beautiful American Cemetery of Florence.

I toured Siena, Lucca, Rome, Perugia and Assisi and then escaped the heat of the summer in Massa Marittima at a monastery where the British Institute offered me more courses in The Art and History of Medieval Tuscany and Beginning Italian (I was a failure at the *Centro di Cultura*). Still not fluent at the end of the summer, I went to Venice for a month to enjoy the film festival, the seafood and the gondola races.

Two-thirds of the way through my "semester" I knew very little Italian, a lot about Italian food, and I had toured every major museum between Rome and Venice. But I still only had a very narrow understanding of Italian culture—the insight of a curious visitor.

Then I finally made some Italian friends. Having discovered that getting to know Florentines is a lot like the societal rules described in a Regency romance—you can't waltz with someone until a mutual friend introduces you, vouching for your good character. I finally was invited into the Florence parallel to the one populated by millions of tourists. Once I befriended one Florentine, I was introduced into a huge circle of family and friends, all who accepted me immediately, no matter how badly I mangled their language.

The Italian Life Rules are serious business, honed over centuries, changing with the times, but in some ways not changing at all. A tourist can be bemused or frustrated by the effect of the rules without learning the cultural significance of the practice. Only an Italian can explain the reason certain things must be done in a certain way. Only the study of the history, art and literature of Italy shows the antecedents of the present day Life Rules.

Over 15 years later, I was still living in Florence, even closer to the Duomo. Now I know so much more about the Italian Life Rules and the Italian Food Rules. I can't claim to have a perfect understanding of any of the rules, but I know for a certainty that they exist and are followed. I haven't adopted many of them, clinging stubbornly to my role as *L'Americana*. This amuses some of my Florentine friends and frustrates others. I wouldn't have it any other way.

Ann Reavis
Florence, 2014

# ALLORA

In Italy, when a person has no idea what to say, they usually start with "*allora*." It buys them time. Most Italian words have strict boundaries of meaning. *Allora* is the epitome of versatility. It conforms itself to almost any scenario. *Allora* has the following meanings: "then", "well then", "in that case", "thus", "therefore", and "so".

In reality, the meaning of the word depends on who you are and how you say it. In Italy, when a teacher yells "*allora*!" it means you'd better sit up and shut up. There is a certain power in the expression, especially when it's accompanied by an exclamation point. *Allora* followed by a comma, however, tells the listener to relax, a story is about to begin.

When I say "*allora*" it is usually accompanied by a question mark. I haven't understood what was said, but I don't want to admit it. What I mean is "*allora?*" or "cut to the chase" or "the bottom line is" or "in sum."

When an Italian says "*allora*" it means he is getting to the point. Pay attention, a plausible explanation may

169

be provided. It is "let's see now" and "let's get to the bottom of this." *Allora* was "what do you think? and "where do we go from here?"—the culmination of a job.

At the end of each of the Italian Life Rules—***Allora:***—will sum up the rule and, perhaps, provide a bit of guidance for your next visit to Italy.

# LA FAMIGLIA

**Heard in Arezzo:** "But I always have lunch with my family on Sunday."

Italians vie for first place with the Japanese regarding the strength of family ties. Love, loyalty, and good behavior among family members are all important. The Italian family comes before city, region or country. It is the DNA of Italian identity.

The benefits of a culture rooted in *la famiglia* are many. It provides a sense of security, a sense of history, a sense of place, a code of conduct, and in many cases a road to success and great wealth. The best run, most profitable businesses in Italy are private family-owned companies—Barilla (pasta), Alessi (home ware), Lavazza (coffee), Ferrero (chocolate), Versace (clothing), and Berlusconi (media and soccer club), among many others.

The Renaissance reached its height through the familial patronage of the Medici, Este, Sforza, and Gonzaga clans. The power of the Renaissance families was

171

based in part on the "five son" philosophy—each family within the clan must produce five sons: one to run the family business; one for the military; one with a political career; one enters the church, hopefully to become a pope; and a spare to replace a fallen sibling. Daughters were also needed to make advantageous marriages to strengthen business, military or political ties. Today, the family in Italy is still strong, but under threat, mainly because the "five son" philosophy has been discarded for an "only child" plan. The values such as loyalty still run strong, but the family trees are now slender saplings, not strong oaks.

The problem with *la famiglia* is that it creates a fragmented society, afraid of change. It worked well in the age of city-states, but now Italy is a country (albeit a young country of just over 150 years). Italians do not have a national identity, except when it comes to the World Cup Soccer Finals. They hardly have a regional identity—see how the Florentines despise the Sienese and the Pisans, and vice versa. Most citizens feel loyalty to their town or city, but look at Siena the animosity between neighborhoods is on display during the Palio race every year.

Italians do not easily leave their family home and rarely move away from their hometown. Studies show that only one in five has moved from one house to another (even in the same town) in the last ten years. Unmarried children (especially boys) do not leave their parental home until late in their 30s, if at all.

Italians will give wholehearted support to the family business and individual family members, but in modern times they do not see the benefit in philanthropy or volunteerism. Great artworks and architecture, underwritten by private wealth is a practice of the distant past. The cultural patrimony (sculpture, museums, theater and opera) is crumbling because there is no value placed on private support for culture and the arts. The same is true of social services and education—no wing of a hospital or library of a university is funded by or bears the name of one of the many wealthy families of the last century.

***Allora:*** Strong family ties may be comforting around the Italian dinner table, but they are strangling Italy's political and economic strength.

# Marriage to the Girl Next Door

**Heard in Siena:** "I can't imagine why you would consider marrying a Florentine."

Many years ago there was a study undertaken to determine what makes a happy and healthy Italian marriage. The results were not a surprise to most Italian mothers with the treasured only son.

The study showed that the best marriages were those between partners who had grown up in the same town. The next happiest were those born and raised in the same region—say a Florentine woman who married a man from Montalcino (caveat: some regional matches per se would never work because of hundreds of years of historical antipathy (Florence/Siena, Florence/Pisa, or Siena/Livorno)).

The shocker to everyone (except the grandmothers) was that it would be better for your Roman son to marry a girl from New York or Stockholm, than to get hitched to a girl from Venice or Milan. International couplings were stronger and happier than interregional pairings.

So why is this?

The first two categories—intercity and intraregional are fairly easy to understand. If the happy couple grew up in the same town, they understand each other completely. Their mothers cooked from the same recipes, the couple supported the same soccer team, and they vacationed every August on the same beach (they probably had their first kiss on that beach). The children from families originating in the same region also ate the same food, had identical philosophies toward housecleaning and child rearing, and also vacationed on the same beach.

Italy is a young country. Just over 150 years ago it was a collection of city-states, each with its own cuisine, its own literature, its own dialect, its own thousand years of history, in short, its own cultural personality. So even with a shared national language (that many grandparents do not speak to this day) and a general love of pasta, no man is going to think his wife, born and bred in another region, can cook fish, vegetables, or pasta sauce as good as his mother.

Because they see themselves as Italian, couples from two different regions expect that they will have common housekeeping rules, social behavior, and ways of dealing with money. But they won't. They won't honor the same saints, cheer for the same team, or agree on the same destination for summer vacation.

If your spouse, however, comes from another

country, there are no expectations. For years, every difference will get a pass. *La Mamma* will try to educate her daughter-in-law, but she will forgive most failings of a foreign spouse, avoiding a battle royal.

**Allora:** If the foreign spouse is the husband, his new Italian wife and her mother will get him whipped into shape in no time and he will learn to love the process. He will certainly love the food.

# MAMMA'S BOYS

**Heard in Naples:** "As soon as I finish cooking your lunch I will do your laundry, my darling boy."

Currently eight out of ten Italians under the age of 30 live at their mother's home and the average age for moving out is 36. Men make up the bulk of those staying at home, at around 70 percent, and a mocking phrase has even been coined to describe them: "*mammoni*" or "big mamma's boys".

Many a foreign girlfriend has learned to her sorrow that her incredibly romantic boyfriend, the man she hopes to marry, is hopelessly addicted to his mother. A foreign woman will probably meet her Italian boyfriend in a bar or restaurant. She won't know where he lives for months and then she won't know that he is using the same single bed that he has slept on since he was six. She may not meet his family until he proposes.

Italian girls are familiar with the *mammoni* phenomenon. An Italian woman will have met her future husband through an introduction from a mutual friend or she will have grown up next door to his parents' home or she will have met him at the same beach where her family and his spend each summer. Italian girls know that the guy they are dating lives at home and will continue to live there until they are married. At that point, the Italian girl assumes they will take up residence within a mile of her mother-in-law.

Some cite the high cost of living and lack of jobs for the *mammoni* cultural norm. The average wage for Italians aged between 25 and 30 is only half of what their peers in England or Germany earn, so it is difficult for them to find their own homes. Financial problems, however, don't plague most of the *mammoni*. They have jobs, disposable income, girlfriends, and frequently, they buy their own apartment (in the same neighborhood as the rest of the family). They just prefer to live at home where their mother cooks, cleans, shops, and worries about them. They continue to be the little *principe* long into their 30s and 40s. What's not to like?

An Italian girl is expected to work as hard as her mother around the family home. This is probably why Italian women move out sooner than their brothers.

Many worry that because young Italians are staying at home, the country is losing out on its growth potential and innovation. The *mammoni* make little movement either geographically, socially or professionally and have no propensity to take risks. Many *mammoni*, those who have gone away to school or moved across town, happily send their laundry home to their mothers, and studies show that over 40 percent, when they do finally move out, rent or buy homes less than a mile from their parents.

Some don't place the blame on the young Italians, but rather on their "clingy parents" who don't let their sons move out. These parents use their extra income to bribe them into staying at home. The unmarried *mammone* will never leave home until his mother demands a grandchild and then it will still seem that he never left home at all.

A British woman on the day of her engagement sat down with her future mother-in-law and had the following conversation:

"I will let you marry my son," said *La Mamma*, "if he comes to my house for dinner once a week so that I know he is going to get at least one good meal *and* I will continue to do his laundry."

The English girl thought, "Yes, she has denigrated my cooking skills, but one meal per week will be a nice break and the laundry offer is a win-win." To show she wasn't a wimp, she counter-offered, "You can have his laundry with my thanks, but the weekly meal has to be lunch, not dinner."

Her future mother-in-law smiled. "Welcome to the family."

Within six months, the marriage was on the rocks. The *mammone* was eating every lunch with his parents and complaining about how the dinner menu was not to his usual standards. His mother had a key to the new couple's apartment, so that she could gather his laundry and used this as an excuse to snoop and comment. The *mammone* would excuse his mother, "It's just her way," he'd say with a shrug. "Just ignore her. You know she means well." Recent statistics show that interfering mothers-in-law were responsible for 30 percent of all marital separations.

In 2014, over 60 percent of Italians, aged 18 to 29, live with their parents. On the one hand the "children" may want to prolong their adolescence, while their parents are pleased to be needed, but if they don't resolve their parental relationship it will be impossible to establish a deep connection with a partner and start a new family.

**Allora:** Many foreign girls dream of traveling to Italy and finding devastatingly romantic man who resembles Michelangelo's *David* to marry and live with "happily ever after." If *La Mamma* resides within 100 miles of the newly minted couple, the dream is likely to turn into a nightmare resemblinging a bad television reality show—*True Lives of Italian Brides.*

# ONE IS ENOUGH

**Heard on the playground:** Silence

The Italian family with six to eight children is a thing of the past. It's a problem. Italians are not having babies. They may be Catholic and the Pope may forbid both birth control and abortion, but the Italian population stopped growing about 50 years ago.

In a country with few children, and fewer playgroups, the treasured only child grows up socializing with adults. Italy has become a country of youngsters with great table manners and an uncertain future.

Mussolini was good at convincing mothers to have babies; it was their patriotic duty. After World War II, the country was impoverished and families could not afford more mouths to feed. But during the boom years of the 50s and 60s, Italy produced a bumper crop of kids. At the same time the agricultural laws changed. The sharecropping system that needed children to work in the fields ended and families moved to the cities to take industrial jobs. Now the former farm help became extra mouths to feed. The one-child family became the norm.

By the 80s, the family could not survive on one income and women joined the workforce. The decision to have a child was delayed to a point that one was all a woman could fit in before the biological clock ticked down.

For many couples, though, being open to having a second child is difficult. First of all, young people often put off becoming married until they have stable jobs that pay well—not an easy task in a country with a high unemployment rate. The high cost of living is also commonly cited as a cause for delayed nuptials, because couples cannot afford to set up house together.

Paradoxically, maternity benefits in Italy are quite generous, by U.S. standards. Women stay home two months before giving birth and three months after while still receiving 80 percent of their salary. Many even manage to take unpaid leave until their child's first birthday.

Similar to their U.S. counterparts, however, Italian women face the challenge of juggling work and family. Some women are fortunate enough to have mothers or mothers-in-law willing to help with child care, but another change to the Italian traditional family ways was the post-war generation of grandmothers not resigned to becoming an unpaid babysitter of the extended family. In the meantime, Italy has not created the childcare support systems common in the neighboring European countries. Private daycare is expensive. A small percentage of Italians who can afford it, turn to nannies or au pairs.

It is not uncommon, though, for a woman, upon returning from maternity leave, to find that her desk has been assigned to someone else and she has been transferred or demoted. Those who have had such an experience after the birth of one child are reluctant to do it again.

There are, of course, women who decide to leave their jobs and become full-time mothers, though the cost of living often precludes this choice. Unlike in the U.S., where it is possible for a woman to quit her job, be a full-time mother for a few years and later re-enter the work force, leaving a good job in Italy often means never finding another one.

As economic times slowed and unemployment rose, women have been discouraged from joining the workforce, men have delayed marrying and continue to live at home late into their 30s. Now immigrants from Eastern Europe, Africa and Asia provide the population growth.

Babies and toddlers in Italy are not treated like the tykes they are. Only children look like tiny adults. They are dressed in designer (or designer knock-off) clothing, identical to their parents and grandparents. Their hair is styled in the manner of the same-sexed adult (gel for boys, accessories for girls). All of this extreme styling will be under layers and layers of outerwear, no matter the time of year.

Only children never get to walk around naked, or

wearing just a diaper, or go barefoot. They are much too fragile and coddled. They are taught that the world is a dangerous place where a gust of air can dive through two layers of clothing to attack an unwary stomach or neck. They learn that a bare foot is only safe under the covers in bed, not on the living room floor or even poolside. The decline in the Italian family size means that there will be proportionately more only children, which conventional wisdom says are lonely, maladjusted and selfish.

In a country where there are more people aged 80 than aged 10 the future is murky. For one thing, Italy's unspoken social contract between young and old is being mangled, if there are not enough young around to pay the old ones' pensions (and immigration is no long-term answer: immigrants' birth rates generally fall, often in less than a generation, to match that of their host country. Then the newcomers grow old—and the birth dearth returns).

***Allora:*** This century will be one where *la famiglia* becomes a weaker force. Family bonds are already growing more complex, as people cohabit, divorce or set up home with partners of the same sex. (Same sex partners are not allowed to adopt in Italy.) Many Italians, who have no siblings, will reach the end of their lives with no immediate relatives at all.

# A COUNTRY OF ELDERS

**Heard in Montefalco:** "*Buon compleanno, Nonna!*"

In 2013, hundreds of villagers gathered in the church of a tiny Sardinian town for a mass to celebrate the 100th birthday of Claudina Melis. But she was not the first to reach that milestone. Next to her in the front pew was her 105-year-old sister, Consolata. Nearby sat five other Melis siblings, all older than 85. The year before, the Melis family entered the Guinness Book of World Records for having the highest combined age of any nine living siblings on Earth—more than 825 years. Sustained by good genes, fresh air, a Mediteranian diet, lots of physical exercise and powerful family bonds, the Melises have become elderly symbols of a way of life that is the envy of the world.

Only the Japanese have a longer life expectancy than Italians. With older people in Italy living longer and longer lives—and with fertility rates low and youth unemployment soaring—experts warn that Italy's demographic crisis is exacerbating a growing debt crisis. In the coming years, they warn, there will be fewer workers paying into the social security system to support the generous pensions of older generations.

Between 2001 and 2011, the number of centenarians in Italy rose 138 percent, and that of nonagenarians, or people in their 90s, rose 78 percent. In 2011, the most recent year in the official statistics, 20 percent of Italians were over the age of 65.

In 2014, Italy's youth unemployment rate was near 40 percent. Many qualified Italians leave for better jobs abroad in a brain drain that weighs on the country's mood and economy. There are small isolated towns that are solely populated by elders as the young leave for bigger cities to find jobs.

Italy is becoming a country of old men and women. The strain is great on the only children, born in the 50s and 60s as part of the one child phenomenon that occurred after World War Two, who are now reaching retirement age with the lonely responsibility for caring for parents in their eighties and nineties. These retirees wonder who is going to care for them in 20 years when over 10 percent of Italy's population will be over 80-years old.

***Allora:*** Riding through a hill town in Tuscany, a tourist snaps a photo of four very old men sitting outside the local coffee bar and does not realize that this is not only a quaint snap-shot, but is also a symbol of Italy's future.

# To *Ciao* or Not to *Ciao*

**Heard in Rome:** "*Ciao*, Beppe! Is this your mother? *Buonasera*, Signora Orsini."

Who would have thought using a ubiquitous Italian word in Italy could get you into so much trouble. The word is "*ciao*" and if you use it at the wrong time with the wrong person you will leave a lasting negative impression.

*Ciao* is described as the Italian version of "aloha," meaning both "hello" and "goodbye," so how can that be bad? As with many things in Italy, it all comes down to history.

*Ciao* comes from Venetian dialect, where the phrase *s-ciào vostro* meant, "I am your slave." Often, *s-ciào vostro* was shortened to simply *s-ciào* and then to *ciào*. In Latin, the word is *sclavus* and in standard Italian *schiavo*, which is where the Venetian *s-ciào* is derived.

In the 17th century, servants when encountering their employer used the term: "I am your slave." This transformed into "I am your servant," used by a person of inferior social status to one of greater importance and finally, to "I'm at your service" when addressing a stranger of one's own age or older. It was never used as a casual greeting before the 20th century.

In modern Italy, *ciao* is mainly used in informal settings, i.e., among family members, relatives, and friends. In other words, with those one would address with the familiar *tu* (second person singular) as opposed to *Lei* (courtesy form).

With family and friends, *ciao* is the norm even as a morning or evening salutation, in lieu of *buongiorno* or *buonasera*. When used in other contexts, *ciao* may be interpreted as slightly flirtatious, or a request for friendship or closeness. Or it may seem to the recipient as an ill-bred form of address.

Some say that Ernest Hemingway introduced the word *ciao* to the American lexicon in 1929 in his book *A Farewell To Arms* with its Italian setting. Others say it traveled outside of Italy with waves of immigrants after WWI and WWII. Now, it is used throughout the globe as a salutation a greeting, both in writing and speech.

In Italy, however, it is still a *very* informal greeting. To use it with a stranger or an elder is an easy and unknowing way to offend. It is much better to get into practice before you arrive with the proper mode of greeting an Italian and then the salutation to be used when parting company. This is also important when saying goodbye when you are talking on the telephone with a stranger. Never say, "*Ciao.*"

When you are introduced or encounter a stranger,

use the words *buongiorno* (good day) or *buonasera* (good evening), depending on the time of day (*buongiorno* before 1pm and *buonasera* after 1pm). These will become your favorite words because they will never offend and they can be used as both greetings or parting words. If you want to up your game a bit then *piacere* (my pleasure) is a good formal greeting (but never used for parting ways).

Finally, if you would like to split the difference, *salve* is a great greeting for a stranger or a friend, of your age or younger. *Salve* comes from the Latin verb *salvere* (literally, to be well, to be in good health). It can be very friendly, e.g. *Salve! Come va?* (literally, Hi! How's it going?), but on its own it's also a polite form of greeting without being too formal. It is commonly used as a form of salutation, (in fact the word salutation itself comes from the same root: *salute*). So, for example, when you are out walking in the countryside and you meet somebody you don't know *salve* is a very good alternative to *buongiorno*. Like *ciao*, *salve* can be used at any time of the day, but *salve* cannot be used when parting.

When parting company, the safest word to use is *arrivederci*. Like *salve* it can be used with strangers. The formal version is *arrivederla*, which is wise to use with older strangers, priests, nuns, and people in authority. You may wish to start out with *arrivederla* and wait until the person you're talking with tells you that it is too formal. (Permission to move to a more informal form of address always flows downhill from the person in the more elevated social position or older than you.)

*Arrivederci* and *arrivederla* only mean goodbye – not hello – so you can't use them to start a conversation, only to end one.

Americans have become famous for their "Have a nice day!" parting exclamation. Italians use "*buona giornata*" ([have a] good day) less frequently, but it is gaining popularity and can be used with most everyone except the most formal of folks. It is always used as a parting. *Buona serata* ([have a] good evening) is similar, but used usually when parting with someone who is going off to do something fun, for example, an evening at the theater, disco, or cinema.

Does this mean you can never say "*ciao*?" No, you will hear *ciao* being said all over Italy. But if you pay close attention, you'll see that it's almost always used between people who know one another or are in the same peer group. Among strangers, or when addressing an elder or someone in a more senior position, most Italians typically choose *salve* or some other more formal greeting.

**Allora:** When in doubt, don't say "*Ciao.*"

# TO KISS THE OTHER CHEEK

**Seen in Venice:** Two Americans trying to shake hands and kiss cheeks at the same time.

Who would have thought an innocent gesture of goodwill could cause so much confusion among friends, family and associates? When to kiss, how many kisses, left cheek, right cheek, both cheeks, lips or not? Visitors to Italy often have cheek kissing anxiety.

Have you ever greeted an Italian by going for a cheek kiss only to have them extend an arm for a hearty handshake and a cheery, "*Buongiorno*" or "*Piacere?*" Regions and cultures often dictate kissing rules, but the bottom line to the kissing dilemma is this: When in doubt, don't!

Some things to consider before offering a cheek include how well you know the person, whether it is a business or social occasion, and your own motive behind the gesture. Keep in mind that much of this depends on the personality of the kisser. Most Italians are warm and demonstrative. They particularly enjoy bestowing their kisses on close friends and family, but for new acquaintances (potential future friends), in business settings, and with strangers, a handshake is the greeting of choice.

Don't kiss someone you have never met before. Be a consistent kisser. If you greet someone with a kiss, don't forget to do the same to say, "*Arrivederci.*" Offering your hand for a handshake after a hello kiss sends a confusing message.

If you have a sufficiently close cheek-to-cheek relationship, then start on the right and graze the cheek of the other person with your own, refrain from making the "*Moi, Moi*" or any other sound into the other person's ear. Then switch to the left cheek and repeat. Not to make this difficult, but you may find that in some parts of Italy they start left cheek first and then right. When in doubt, pause and follow the lead of your Italian friend.

Stop at a kiss to each cheek. Unlike in France or Russia, a third pass is extremely rare in Italy. Don't actually kiss the cheek unless it is a very, very close friend or family member. If your kiss includes a hug, make it brief, a few short taps on the back are appropriate, avoid pounding the back of the other person.

Usually the cheek kissing routine is between women and women and men and women, but there are regions in Italy, mostly in the south, where men greet one another with kisses on either cheek. Some suggest that Italian women who wanted their men to sympathize with their suffering when brushing up against scruffy, unshaven beards started this. The safest route for a man visiting Italy is to offer a handshake to greet other men. After that follow the lead of those Italian metrosexual friends. As a general rule, women have the universal power to dictate proximity. The woman has to take charge to avoid any awkwardness.

Ironically, the number one situation most fraught with danger is when a foreigner meets a fellow expat. If the person is a friend, or a friend of a friend, do you stay with the custom of Italy or fall back on the etiquette of the homeland? It's probably safest to stay with the handshake until your relationship rises to the level of closeness that calls for kisses.

***Allora:*** When in doubt, stick with your own cultural norm. There is no need to become Italian in all ways when visiting the country.

# TO SEE AND BE SEEN

**Heard in Matera:** "Where have you been? I haven't seen you at *la passeggiata* for a week."

It used to be that in every city in Italy, every neighborhood had a *piazza*. Every small town had a central *piazza*. Once upon a time the piazza was a place for all of the inhabitants of a town or neighborhood to meet for the *passeggiata*. On the *piazza* or just off the square, you could buy virtually everything you needed to fix meals or eat out, a full range of items for decorating or fixing the home, sufficient clothing for your family, newspapers and magazines, stamps and cigarettes, and a cup of coffee. Today, the piazzas are surrounded by over-priced eateries with food of questionable quality and hotels. Italians now shop at outlying supermarkets and go to the mall for everything else.

Italy hasn't quite perfected the mall. The present ones are a strange marriage of the American strip mall of small shops ringing a parking lot and the outlet mall that hasn't figured out how to discount prices. The social life of the American mall has yet to arrive in Italy

197

where the *passeggiata* of the piazza moves inside.

What is *la passeggiata*?

As evening falls and the harsh sun inches out of the piazza, an evening ritual begins, the Italian tradition of *la passeggiata*, a gentle stroll (this is not a brisk walk) through the main streets of the old town, usually in the pedestrian zones in the *centro storico*, the historic center. The piazza may not be the same, but *la passeggiata* will never die.

This evening promenade, generally between 5 and 8 pm, occurs in virtually every town, village, or big city in Italy. During the week, the *passeggiata* marks the end of the workday and offers a moment of sociability before the family dinner. The *passeggiata* is especially popular on Saturday and Sunday evenings. During the summer, some Italians even drive to nearby cities, the coast, or the lakes for a special *passeggiata*. It is a family affair.

*Andiamo a fare qualche vasca!* (Let's go do some laps!), Italians in the south say to one another. However, this cultural performance involves much more than strolling to and fro. Italians tend to dress up for the *passeggiata*. Tourists are easy to spot in their shorts, flip-flops and fanny packs. Older denizens sit along the route, nursing a beer or a glass of wine in the bar, and watching for things to gossip about; *la passeggiata* is where new romances are on display, as well as new babies and new shoes. The most important thing is simply seeing and being seen. For townspeople of all ages, the *passeggiata* reinforces a sense of belonging, largely lost in other countries.

**Allora:** The *passeggiata* is a great way to observe Italians when they are happiest and most comfortable. Dress up and join the parade.

# LOVE AND DATING ITALIAN STYLE

**Heard in Florence:** "Italian men are the world's best lovers and the world's worst husbands."

Italian men are born to seduce, they are raised to seduce (taught by their fathers and practicing their lines on their mothers), and they spend their lives seducing every single woman they meet (the 95-year old on his last day of life will die while trying to seduce the nurses in the hospital). This does not mean they go through with it, they just practice the art of seduction on all the women they meet, single, married, old or young. Once they are married they continue to seduce every woman they meet, except their wife, who now becomes a hybrid of the Madonna and their mother.

When romancing a woman, an Italian man's instinct is to be as aggressive as possible. Not in a threatening way, but to shower her with compliments and profess his eternal love and admiration until she believes at least half of what he is saying. Then he knows the game is won. When dealing with any Anglo-Saxon woman (American, British, Australian, or Canadian), the Italian man does not even break a sweat. He knows that they are so unused to blatant flattery, unimagined promises, and the concept of eternal love that he will have them in bed within a day or two; perhaps within an hour or two, but what is the challenge in that? His goal is sex, not some ill-defined forever.

Italian women are born to resist seduction. Unlike their Anglo-Saxon sisters, they have watched this game since the day they started to walk. They know that a woman's job is to resist as aggressively as possible. To do otherwise would put her virtue in question. The would-be Romeo is rebuffed, scoffed at, or else just ignored outright. The Italian woman knows every move an Italian man can bring to the tournament of love. She has learned watching her mother. She knows the perils of empty promises and talk of forever.

To gain her favor, the Italian man has to try a little harder. Smooth talk alone doesn't warrant her attentions – she gets that from every *ragazzo* and old man in town. Sincerity might catch her off guard, but probably earning potential and consistency will win her heart. Italian women, like Eve, look to get out of the garden and into the real world. They are cynics at heart.

Female visitors to Italy are either doomed to be heartbroken, or if they are made of tougher stuff, they will have the romantic adventure of their lives. Old, young, gorgeous or plain, these traveling Janes will be pampered; sweet talked in perhaps two languages (or at least Italian); offered any enticement (some obtainable); and, if lucky, may have the best sex they've had to date. Or not. Italian men are world-class at the seduction, but may fall short or fade fast at the finish line. And unless this is a very unusual Italian man, forget about forever. If you are a tourist, the probability that he is married is better than 50 percent. (If you are a James, not a Jane, and looking for love with an Italian man, be warned, he is probably married.)

Anglo-Saxon men in search of an Italian woman may or may not have an advantage. Having been brought up in a politically correct society, where equality between the sexes is valued, he is tongue-tied when it comes to sweet-talking an Italian girl and not just by the language barrier. An Italian woman brought up on the sweet nothings of her compatriot lotharios will find the visiting suitor either boring or pathetic, unless he comes up with an exciting date idea or an innovative gift.

Anglo-Saxon men also have another strike against them—fashion. Even if they make the substantial financial commitment to an Italian wardrobe, it will still not flatter them as it does their Italian competitors. Italian women like the man at their side to look as good as they do.

All is not lost, if the male American or British tourist is looking for a forever partner, he might just get lucky with simple sincerity and a promise of a secure future filled with love, fidelity, and a mostly absent mother-in-law. (It's a better deal than she is getting from her countrymen.) But if he is just as lascivious as his Italian counterpart, albeit dressed as a Puritan, a prepster or a beach bum, then he is out of luck and should search for sex in another country.

***Allora:*** A visitor to Italy from any country outside those that speak a Romance language (French, Italian, Spanish, Portuguese, and Romanian) should never forget that love and dating in Italian may be romantic, but the sweet phrases should be filtered through a fine mesh of skepticism.

# SWEARING IN ANOTHER LANGUAGE

**Heard in Orvieto:** "*Che palle*, Bruno. Give me a break."

After living for a few months in a foreign country, you gain a new and profound appreciation for the minutiae of communicating across languages. You soon discover that the cultural context adds yet another layer of complexity and so there are limitless opportunities for misunderstandings that transcend mere differences in vocabulary, grammar, and pronunciation.

In Italy, *parolacce* (dirty words) are common in everyday speech. With such a rich history of swearing, Italy has scholars of *turpiloquio*, the formal term for foul language because of the infinite variety of Italian vulgarities. Unlike English speakers, Italians use sexual obscenities rather than scatological ones. There are literally hundreds of suggestive words, euphemisms and vulgarities for everything related to sex. The

Ann Reavis

*Dizionario storico del lessico erotico italiano* (Historic Dictionary of the Erotic Italian Lexicon) lists 3,500 *parolacce*.

Take the word "*Vaffanculo*". Many debate the subtle variations of a direct translation, but it is essentially equivalent to the imperative phrase, "go f\*#k yourself" in English. To an American, there really isn't any sweet, gentle way to spin this expression. Unless the speaker is a rap star or a Hollywood agent, it is always an insult at best; and at worst, an invitation to a fight. Of course to the same American, the Italian word sounds warm and friendly. And as in Hollywood, in Italy the *vaffanculo* is used as an endearment, a threat and a part of speech.

In Italy, there was even a V-Day when about half of the country said, "*Vaffanculo*" to the federal government, in good humored resignation.

Expletives in a foreign language don't really touch us viscerally—it's more like being privy to an inside joke. But when an Italian says in English "Go f\*#k yourself," there is no other way to take it. And even though you explain to an Italian that the F-word is offensive—always—they just don't understand the reason why. The same should go for the visitor to Italy. If Italian doesn't trip off the foreigner's tongue with ease, swearing should not be part of any conversational attempt.

***Allora:*** The Italian language is full of hidden traps. Keep in mind the following:

*Penna* means "pen" but if it is spelled or pronounced "*pene*", it means penis. So be very careful with your pronunciation, really stress that second "n." *Penne* is a type of pasta. Again, stress that second "n."

*La scopa* is the Italian word for broom (and a popular game of cards) or can be slang for the sex act.

*Fichi* is the correct terms for figs, as in the fruit, but if pronounced singularly with the "a" at the end instead of the proper "o" (*fico* is one fig) it means a woman's private parts.

*Pisolino* is a cute word for a nap in Italian, but be careful to pronounce this one exactly as written with that long "o" in the middle. If you get lazy, you might be saying "*pisellino*," which literally means "small penis."

*Preservativi* looks like "preservatives," but actually means "condom." Probably you don't want to say that you don't want condoms in your food. Instead, *conservanti* is the word for preservatives.

*Scoraggiare* means "don't give up!" But *scoreggiare* (change one letter) is the verb "to fart."

*Pecorino* is a popular delicious sheep's milk cheese. *Pecorina* means sex, doggy-style.

*Topa* is a female mouse, but is also a euphemism for a lady's genitals.

*Uccello* means "bird" and is also a vulgar term for "penis".

# LET THE HANDS DO THE TALKING

**Seen in Naples:** Thumb to nose, with remaining fingers vertically extended and wagging.

Italians are famous for "talking" with their hands. They are often more expressive in silence than in words. Sometimes it is unseen emphasis as when talking on their cellphones (especially in "hands free" mode). But they are also able to multitask with gestures while smoking a cigarette, eating a piece of pizza or downshifting a car through rush-hour traffic.

Everyone knows the classic fingers pinched against the thumb that can mean "Whaddya mean?" or "I wasn't born yesterday." The world has adopted the open hands that ask, "What's happening?" Hands placed in prayer become a sort of supplication, a rhetorical question: "What do you expect me to do about it?" or "What do you mean?" and a flick of the fingers out from the chin is a bit rude: "I don't care." The world has adopted the shrugged shoulders and two raised hands that say, "Who knows?"

A hand circled slowly, may indicate, "Whatever"

or "That'll be the day," more eloquently than words. Some gestures are simple: the palm of the hand against the belly means hungry; the index finger "screwed" into the cheek means something tastes good; fingers brushing the chin, indicating "I don't give a damn," the classic brushoff; and tapping one's wrist is a universal sign for "hurry up." Pressing the thumb and index finger of one hand together and drawing a straight horizontal line in the air expresses "*Perfetto!*" ("Perfect!").

In Italy, children and adolescents gesture, the elderly gesture, and so does everybody in between. Recently, Italy's highest court ruled that a man who inadvertently struck an 80-year old woman while gesticulating in a piazza in the southern region of Puglia was liable for civil damages, but in 2008, when Umberto Bossi, the colorful founder of the conservative Northern League, raised his middle finger during the singing of Italy's national anthem, prosecutors in Venice determined that the gesture, while obscene and the cause of widespread outrage, was not a crime.

Gestures have long been a part of Italy's political theater. Former Prime Minister Silvio Berlusconi is a noted gesticulator. In a photo op with world leaders he held two fingers behind President Obama's head. To Americans it denotes bunny ears or devil's horns; to Italians it is "*fare le corna*" or a sign that the person is a cuckold.

Americans "flip the bird" and give someone the finger. The equivalent gesture in Italy is more forceful: Men clench the right fist and jerk the forearm up while slapping the right bicep with the left palm (this is rarely seen as a female gesture). It is considered both rude and obscene and often leads to a fight unlike the less emphatic middle finger.

Expert on gestures have identified around 250 gestures that Italians use in everyday conversation. As with most things Italian, gestures have a rich history. One theory holds that Italians developed them as an alternative form of communication during the centuries when they lived under foreign occupation—by Austria, France and Spain in the 14th through 19th centuries—as a way of communicating without their overlords understanding. Over the centuries, the Italian language has evolved, but gestures have remained relatively unchanged.

Books, from the scholarly (i.e., Andrea de Jorio's 1832 treatise *La mimica degli antichi investigata nel gestire napoletano* [The Body Language of the Ancients as Interpreted in Neapolitan Gesture] and Bruno Munari's 1994 *Dizionario dei gesti italiani*) to the helpful English travel guide (also by Munari) interpret Italian hand gestures.

***Allora:*** If a visitor to Italy wants to join the conversation that is not spoken, a bit of study and practice is advised, because what means "Hook'em Horns" to a University of Texas alumnus means something completely different in Italy.

# KEEPING IN TOUCH ITALIAN STYLE

**Heard in front of the Florence Duomo:** "*Che mangi per pranzo?*"

At any one time during waking hours about 80 percent of Italians are talking on their cell phones. They are good texters, but they are better talkers. Seemingly, 90 percent of those conversations are about food—what they ate for the previous meal, what they plan to or wish to eat for the next meal, and how best to prepare the pasta sauce or the main dish for either the past meal or the upcoming feast—and who can blame them?

The other ten percent of the conversations will be evenly split between family matters, health concerns, love, and business. (Perhaps it is about the health concerns brought on by the passionate affair between two people employed by the family business.)

Italians are far behind the rest of the developed world (and some of the emerging economies) when it comes to internet commerce, but they were early-adopters of cell phones. They use very expensive smartphones to call, text, take photos, but use none of the other functions.

Part of the reason for the enthusiasm for cells phones was the continued inefficiency of landline phone providers and the dearth and expense of public phones. But the main reason for a cell phone (or two) carried by every Italian is that they love to talk and be connected. To Italians, silence is not golden.

Having someone to call is not a problem. *La Mamma* wants to hear from you at least twice a day (after each meal) if you don't live with her, and at least once a day if you do. Your father, siblings, grandparents, lovers, colleagues and friends all expect their portion of your calling day.

Cell phones have also freed up Italian hands and arms to join in the conversation. With a simple earbud and microphone, an Italian is free to be as expressive as possible without getting a neck ache from cradling the landline phone. On the street it may seem like Italy is a country of schizophrenics talking to invisible "others", but to Italians it's true freedom of expression.

The problem of cell phones in a country of 700-year old stone buildings is one of signal. It is frequently impossible to send or receive a call inside your place of business, thus creating a country of shopkeepers standing on the curb sharing their views on food, family, health, love and business with the occupants of the apartments directly above their heads.

**Allora:** Even if a tourist buys an I
use in the phone he brought from hom
function due to the cell phone being "
high cost of "roaming charges" can cause post-vaca-
tion regret. Many times it is easier and cheaper to buy
a simple disposable phone and SIM card on the first
day of your holiday to keep in touch like the Italians
do.

# PASSING THE DINING TABLE EXAM

**Heard after Sunday lunch in Florence:** "Did the *ossobuco* have too much salt?"

Italians are serious about food and they have every right to be. They are world-class experts. Every meal provides an opportunity for comment and critique, be it at home or in a restaurant. Italians are brutally honest during the after-dinner comment period. They did not learn from Thumper's mother, "If you don't have something nice to say, don't say anything at all." There is no glossing over defects, even if your own mother did the cooking.

The catch for the foreigner or the unwary is that you must earn the right to comment. You do not have to prove your *bona fides* if: 1) you were born and bred in Italy to Italian parents; 2) you are of Italian heritage and have returned to the motherland for a sufficient period of time (one to two uninterrupted years); or 3) you are a foreigner who can actually cook and has lived in Italy for at least a decade. Otherwise, you must prove that your understanding of the Italian Food Rules and Italian cuisine is beyond reproach through a long and serious practical exam, overseen by experts.

Let's take a virtual look-see at a hapless foreigner, Bill Brown, who, after months, has finally been invited by a Florentine friend to join her family for Sunday lunch at her parents' home.

"*Beel*," says *La Mamma*, peering at him across the table, "what did you think of my *spaghetti alle vongole*?"

"It was delicious," says Bill. "Best I ever had."

"You didn't think," she starts and then pauses, "it was lacking salt. The sauce was a bit *sciocca*?"

"No, it was perfect, plenty of salt."

"I also thought the pasta noodles were *scotti*— oo soft, overcooked. What did you think?"

By this time Bill's friend tries to come to the rescue. "*Mamma, basta, per favore*. What does he know?"

But Bill doesn't see the trap. "No, the pasta had plenty of chew—*al dente*, I think you call it."

*La Mamma* turns to her daughter, Bill's friend, and her husband, who is seriously contemplating the last sip in his wine glass, and says, "Mr. Brown thinks my pasta sauce was too salty and the spaghetti wasn't cooked enough. What do you think?"

Her husband will take that last sip of wine and Bill's friend will toss him into *purgatorio*: "Mamma, what does he know? He's American. He makes *spaghetti alle vongole* with canned clams and you know they always overcook the pasta."

Bill can only make penance and earn his way out of purgatory by eating in silence for a year or two (or ten), observing the experts, before he once again tries to participate in the competitive field of Italian culinary critique.

***Allora:*** The best way to enjoy being Italian for awhile is through eating the local cuisine, but don't try to compete in the so so serious practice of critiquing *La Mamma's* food.

# AT HOME AT THE COFFEE BAR

**Heard at the bar in Parma:** *"Un caffè un cornetto, per favore."*

The concept of going to a bar, and the definition of the bar itself, is very different in Italy than in the U.S or Northern European countries. A bar in Italy is more often a place for coffee than alcohol, although alcoholic beverages can be found at every bar.

On every street there is at least one bar where one can have a quick breakfast in the morning, usually consisting of a coffee or cappuccino and a sweet roll. Throughout the day, the bar usually serves coffees, juices and alcohol as well, but the point is to have a quick stop, rather than hanging out with friends for drink after drink.

Socially, the bar in small towns can be a gathering place, but its structure and its overall concept still remains that of a quick stop, although many elderly might also use it as a place to get together to play cards and talk about sports or politics.

In smaller towns, a main bar in the central square

becomes the meeting point for many, especially for the evening *passeggiata*. In cities popular with tourists, such as Florence, some bars are fancy and big and, in these cases, their function is often to be more of a social place, especially during the summer, when the good weather allows a pleasant outdoor experience: here you'll find many people enjoying a gelato or a cold drink on the piazza. But beware, because to sit at a table in one of these places will triple or quadruple the price of any drink or food item.

Although they never meant to be restaurants, in recent years bars have started to serve food, especially at lunch, and besides fresh sandwiches or *tramezzini*, hot meals are also offered. A bar is a fast way to get fed, without going too far from one's place of work.

Many small bars are family-run and stay open from early morning to the late hours of the evening, and they can also be a quick, last minute shopping place for small items, such as milk or water. In Italy, bars are allowed to sell alcohol to take-away and it is also legal to drink while standing in the street.

In historical piazzas or particularly beautiful areas of the country, coffee bars are located in strategic places where it is possible to enjoy breathtaking sights. A visitor should spend a few hours relaxing and enjoying the view, while keeping in mind that at the prices you're paying you are "renting" the table, so do not rush. Your waiter will not make any effort to move you along.

Bars are also the place for an *aperitivo*. Italians will

gather to a chosen bar after work, again for not for very long, and enjoy a quick drink (just one) before dinner while eating some appetizers. In recent years this has become even more of a trend, and many bars offer a great selection of finger foods, garnering a new name *apericena*, a light dinner.

**Allora:** As a visitor to Italy, the coffee bar is going to be your go-to place for a quick snack, a drink or *cappuccino* (only before 10am), but will also be a spot to meet your Italian friends, ask for directions, and find a toilet (purchase something, first). Away from your hotel or rental apartment, the coffee bar is going to be the most useful public space always available to you.

# THE TOBACCO SHOP HAS IT ALL

**Heard at the Questura:** What do you mean I have to go to the tobacco shop to buy a stamp for 4 euro 67 cents? What kind of stamp?"

In Italy the sale of tobacco is regulated and taxed and this has been so for centuries. Columbus brought the first plants back to Europe in 1492, but it wasn't until the 17th century when tobacco was grown in Tuscany and Umbria, and hand-rolled by women in the area near Lucca, creating the famed Toscano cigar.

Pope Urban VII's 13-day papal reign included the world's first known tobacco use restrictions in 1590 when he threatened to excommunicate anyone who "took tobacco in the *loggia* of or inside a church, whether it be by chewing it, smoking it with a pipe or sniffing it in powdered form through the nose". Pope Urban VII  and his strictures did not last long.

Soon after, various governmental entities started to tax the sale of the addictive product that everyone wanted. (One of the flames that kindled the wars for unification of Italy was the 1848 "tobacco riot" in Milan over high tobacco taxes imposed by the Austrian overlords.) Today, the excise tax is 58.3 percent of the ultimate cost of any tobacco product.

Salt used to be taxed, too. Until 1975, in Italy this tax was collected through fiscal monopolies and the imposition of import customs. The State had a monopoly on the manufacture and sale of salt, and fixed the final market price, which included the tax rate of about 70 percent of the selling price. That is why on many of the *Tabaccaio* signs with their large "T" it reads "*Sali e Tabacchi*" because those were the two most common products controlled by the State. Salt can't be bought at the *Tabaccaio* anymore; try the supermarket. Tobacco, however, is not the only controlled item, which is why lottery tickets, INPS payments (social security payments), postal stamps, bus, metro and train tickets, and tax stamps for government documents (*valori bollati*), all can be obtained at the *Tabaccaio*.

Now the most elegant *Tabaccaios* have a huge selection of cigars from all over the world, including the small pungent *Toscano* or *Toscanello*, as well as cigarettes from a variety of countries (Italy does not have its own cigarette industry). The *Tabaccaio* is still the place to find all of the paraphernalia for smoking.

Your shopping experience need not be limited to tobacco. Even though you can't find salt, you will be able to recharge your cell phone and buy an international phone card. You can find batteries, postcards, water and soda, candy and gum, condoms, jewelry and watches, and sometimes a fully-stocked coffee bar at the local *Tabaccaio*.

**Allora:** One day a popular Italy blogger stopped by her local *Tabaccaio* and asked for twenty postage stamps with which she planned to send her holiday cards. The woman at the register told her that she would sell her 12 stamps because, even though she had about 30 stamps on hand, she didn't want to run out in case someone else wanted to buy some. There was nothing the writer could do to convince the *Tabaccaio* owner that first come, first serve or that replenishing her stock of stamps might be a reasonable alternative.

# SOCCER MANIA

**Heard in Milan:** "For the millions that are paid you would think we could at least beat Juventus."

Whole books can be written about Italy's passion for soccer. So as a small example, it's educational to look at the Vatican's view of the national pastime.

It wasn't surprising when one high-ranking cardinal who is a well-known soccer fan was taken seriously a few years ago when he joked that the Vatican should form its own team. Cardinal Tarcisio Bertone, then Vatican Secretary of State (since retired) and an ardent supporter of Turin's Juventus team, said: "I cannot cross out (the possibility) that in the future the Vatican could set up its own soccer team" on a par with Italy's top soccer leagues. Media outlets ran with the news, even splashing speculation across their pages on who the future Vatican coach might be. A former Italian national team manager, Giovanni Trapattoni, whose sister is a nun, was fingered as a favorite.

Later, the cardinal said his comments had been in jest and turning cleat-clad Vatican soccer players into national competitors was "unfeasible." "We will continue playing our strictly amateur competitions," he said during a tournament that pitted the Swiss Guard against St. Peter's Basilica maintenance workers and another team of the Vatican Museums' staff. The Vatican Museums' team won that tournament.

It wasn't the first time Cardinal Bertone, who occasionally did radio commentary for Division A soccer matches while he was archbishop of Genoa, mused to reporters about a hypothetical Vatican dream team. But he wasn't teasing when, during the summer madness of the World Cup, he pitched a tournament idea to the Catholic Italian Sports Center. He told representatives of the center that Rome's pontifical universities were a unique, untapped treasure trove of future sports heroes. "We in Rome have a great opportunity—if you look at all the pontifical institutes, the entire world is represented all under our own roof." Then came the creation of the Clericus Cup. Seminarians in Rome swapped their cassocks and clerical shirts for soccer jerseys, shorts and matching knee socks. Organizers said they expected the Vatican to hit the pitch and take part in the new amateur sports tournament.

Future priests studying at Rome's pontifical universities, colleges and institutes are invited to form a team and "put themselves back in the game, dribbling, making saves and headers," the Catholic Italian Sports Center website said. Instead of countries pitted one against another, the Vatican saw the opportunity for national loyalties to disappear as African, Asian, European and American seminarians played together under the banner of a love for the sport and the positive values the game fortifies. (Unlike in the professional stadiums where racist behavior mars the image of Italian soccer.)

***Allora:*** For the tourist from a country where soccer mania does not reign, it is absolutely necessary to experience the game in person to understand the Italians' passion for the sport. Arrange to get tickets and go to the stadium at least once during your visit.

(Vatican City is now the smallest sovereign state to field a national soccer team. Outfitted in white and yellow, the team lost to Monaco (2-0) on May 10, 2014.)

# ITALIANS STICK TOGETHER

**Seen at the Vatican:** The line into St. Peter's Basilica with Italians layered together and the American and British standing out to the side, while still maintaining their place in the queue.

Americans, explorers of the wild frontier, owners of an acre of manicured lawn, are physically taller and wider than other nationalities, and generally prefer more personal space than people do in Italy, be it actual feet between individual bodies or yards away from the next-door neighbor's house. Perhaps the Italians' love of closeness stems from their 1,000-year history of city-states, living behind fortified walls for safety's sake. In the U.S. the ideal home is a single-family house surrounded by land. In Italy it is a spacious condominium apartment with a good view. Italians will frequently wonder why anyone would like to live in the countryside.

In the U.S., personal space is very closely linked to ideals of individualism. There's an idea that a person has the right to this space. It is a culture that prizes independence, privacy and capitalism. Italians prize close family ties and friendship. They will often walk arm in arm, touch each other during conversation, and speak face to face. Individualism is not an attribute supported by the society.

It is rare for visitors to have confrontations about personal space. No one will ever turn to the person behind them in line and say 'I like you, but you're standing too close to me,' Rather, Americans will likely angle and inch their bodies away from anyone they feel breached their buffer zone, stick out an elbow or place a shopping bag in the space. Italians don't use the distancing actions of Americans. In Italy, the iPod craze, which turns city streets and commuter trains into islands of individuality, has not occurred.

Despite Italians' outsized fear of germs, they have no sense of personal space. In line at the post office, the man or woman behind you will be pressed up against you. You might think this is a weird sex thing, but really they are just trying to get to the front of the line faster and feel that extra five inches might make the difference. Or perhaps being wise to the working of the "Italian Line," they are afraid some little old lady with a cane will slip in front of them. (They should know that the pensioner with the walking stick is going to go directly to the front of the line before she makes her move.)

In a bus, the crowd near the exit door will be packed like sardines in a can and about as fragrant. On the street, two Italians will be nose to nose in conversation. In a restaurant, the second party to arrive will be seated by the host right next to the only occupied table in the place. Looking for space in an empty movie theater, look in the U.S. In Italy, those arriving after you are sure to sit directly in front of you or in the seat beside you.

***Allora:*** Visitors to Italy should be aware that personal space is not valued by the locals, but should also be alert to the fact that the person behind you in line may not be Italian and may be picking your pocket.

# BEWARE THE DREADED DRAFT

**Heard in the apartment hallway in Rome:** "Leo, come back here immediately. Put on your scarf. Do you want to catch pneumonia?"

In no other part of the world is the air believed to be as dangerous as it is in Italy. Not because of pollution, although cities like Florence have some of the most polluted air in Europe, but because of the air itself—throughout the country—inside and outside. In fact, air seems to be more risky inside than out. Air-conditioned air is the worst of all.

Tell an Italian that you have any of the following symptoms: headache, sore throat, indigestion, chest pain, toothache, earache, stiff neck; and the diagnosis will be the same—you have been attacked by air. Specifically, you have experienced a blast of air or *colpo d'aria*. The incident of exposure could have lasted for a few seconds or for hours, but must have occurred within the last week.

The result of the dreaded draft will be a *cervicale* (sore back), *torcicollo* (stiff neck), *mal di testa* (headache), *raffreddore* (head cold), or *congestione* (cramp anywhere on the body that was exposed to the blast of air). These relatively mild ailments could lead to pneumonia or death.

Not being Italian, the tourist is not in danger of contracting any of these ailments from the *colpo d'aria*. The tourist, instead, will be merely hot because the air conditioning will be off in the car, the train, or the restaurant. Or she will be suffocating because the windows cannot be open at night, or in a car, or in a train.

Alone in a restaurant, trying to cool down on a sweltering hot August day, it is guaranteed that a group of Italians will arrive and within five minutes ask the waiter to turn off the AC "for their health." Refrigerated air is considered more peril-filled than fresh air.

Night air is also considered dangerous to the unwary sleeper, who fails to cover his stomach, back or neck. It is considered safer to keep the windows closed.

Sweaty bodies are especially at risk, as are children emerging from the ocean onto a blistering hot beach. An Italian mother will always have a sweater, scarf, and socks (cotton in summer, wool in winter) in her humongous purse in case her treasured only child is threatened by air.

Only tourists will risk drying their hair *au natural*, either inside or on the street. Only tourists expose their tummies to the errant breeze. At naptime, to protect the delicate stomach from a chill, mother will warn her child or her husband: *"Tesoro, devi coprirti la pancia!"* (You must cover your tummy). Although the midriff-on-view style is currently *la moda*, an Italian woman will be carrying layers of clothing in case the temperature drops a couple of degrees. Italian men may expose too much chest at the collar of a shirt, but there will be a sweater draped over those manly shoulders. Italian men do not go shirtless, except at the beach, and then only if there is no wind.

***Allora:*** The benefit of this fear of a cooling breeze, of course, is that Italy produces the most beautiful scarves, sweaters, wraps, shawls, and other apparel in silk, cotton, cashmere and wool to protect the delicate necks and shoulders from the dreaded draft.

# STAY OFF THE GRASS

**Heard on the side of the road at a panoramic vista of Tuscany:** "I've got folding chairs in the trunk for us to sit on, Mamma."

Only in the direst emergency, or to be polite to a foreigner, will an Italian sit on a floor. If they do lower themselves to that germ- and dust-infested level, they will try to put a layer of cardboard, cloth, or plastic in between them and the ground. The barrier will provide insulation from the potential chill and protection from both pathogens and dust on their clothes.

To a somewhat lesser extent this rule extends to the outdoors where Italians would prefer not to sit on the steps to the museum or church, a curb on a street, or the ground, be it paved or soil. Italians are not given to picnicking on the grass or on a tablecloth spread on *terra firma*. Italians prefer *alfresco* dining at a table or, at least, on chairs.

In Rome, police started to hand out fines to tourists eating lunch while sitting on the Spanish Steps. In Florence, do not try to sip that Coke or munch on a

241

*panino* on the steps of the Duomo or the *pietra serena* benches of the *Loggia dei Lanzi*.

Many Renaissance palaces have a stone bench skirting the edifice. This part of the building was included in the design because noble families wanted the doors to stay shut, keeping out the riffraff, but also wanted the neighbors to see how many people were waiting for banking services, begging for favors, or supporting the political whims of the family inside. Italians today are still willing to rest on these historic benches (usually protected by a sheet of newsprint), but not on the ground below or on the building steps where the shoes of strangers have trod and the dogs of careless owners have piddled or worse.

**Allora:** Visitors to Italy should be aware that what they chose to sit on may be 700-years old and should be treated with respect. Search for a bench in a nearby piazza.

# STAY OUT OF THE WATER

**Heard at the beach in Viareggio:** "Gino, I know that girl is swimming, but she's British. She doesn't know that going in the water right after breakfast can kill you."

Many cultures have the rule "don't go in the water until three hours after you eat." Italians actually follow the rule. To Italians, however, this is not just a poolside or beach prohibition; it extends to immersion into all manner of water.

At the pool or at the beach, the lemming-like masses leave to clean up for lunch at 11:30am and by 12:30pm the pool or the beach will be vacant. A few will return by 3:00pm, but they only plan to stretch out in the shade for a nap.

The rule is reinforced every summer when the Italian TV news reports on at least one or two occasions that a person has died of *congestione*—a blockage of the digestive system that leads to a cramp and resultant drowning.

Concern for digestive health as well as a fear of

*torcicollo* (stiff neck) prevents Italians from showering or bathing after dinner. Everyone knows that all of the blood in the body rushes to the stomach to aid in digestion after a meal. To distract the blood flow to another quadrant of the system is only asking for trouble. They may shower after lunch, but it will be at least three hours after their last bite. They, of course, know that they will not drown or die of bathroom ablutions after meals, but will studiously avoid the very real potential for indigestion or headache brought on by exposure to bath or shower water.

**Allora:** When it comes to *congestione* or *torcicollo*, it seems that the random tourist is not at risk just because he crosses the border into Italy. Just be aware that the Italians are watching out for your health when issuing the warning to stay out of the water.

# Barefoot Peril

**Heard in Verona:** "*Che schifo*! Don't those Australians know that walking around on bare feet can kill you?"

One of the joys of summer in the U.S., Australia, and other countries is the chance to walk outside barefoot. No Italian children will ever know that sense of the warm sidewalk toasting the soles of their feet or newly mown grass tickling their arches or mud squishing between their toes. Even at the beach or on the deck of the public swimming pool, Italians will be wearing the appropriate rubber footwear.

To an Italian mother there are three considerations: First, the chill that a child of any age might contract from cold feet; second, the bacteria, viruses, and fungi that the bare skin might absorb; and third, the esthetic problem of dusty, dirty, or muddy feet. The last concern leads also to the problem of the dirt those bare feet track into the house, so separate at-home footwear (slippers or sandals) is also mandatory.

In Italian cities and towns the citizens have a point: the excrement of dogs, the acceptance of men urinating in corners, and the difficulty faced when trying to clean streets and sidewalks made of ancient stones should discourage even those tourists who would normally walk barefoot in their home country.

To an Italian, walking barefoot in any environment other than their own shower is unthinkable.

***Allora:*** Wear flip-flops if you must, but don't distress the Italians by going barefoot anywhere but on a sandy beach.

# DON'T SWEAT IT

**Heard in Rome:** "*Non sudare*! Slow down, you are going to get a chill."

Tourists arriving in Italy in July and August stare in wonder at Italians who refuse to wear shorts in the city and seem to not sweat. Little do they realize that the Italian child is taught from birth to not sweat. Just joking. Sort of. More precisely, Italian children are encouraged not to sweat. Sweat may lead to a fatal chill. A breeze might catch that drop of sweat on an exposed neck or knee, be followed by a sore neck (progressing to pneumonia) or a leg cramp.

Shorts also are not considered appropriate city clothing, but are only to be worn at the beach. An Italian would prefer to be a little uncomfortable than to break a fashion rule.

You will rarely find an Italian who jogs. It is not because they do not exercise, but they only exercise in a climate-controlled gym where there is no chance of a cooling draft drying the sweat before they have a chance to shower. Italian men do bicycle, but they wear spandex from head to toe with a helmet to protect the sweaty head. A woman or child riding in town will be urged to go at a sedate pace—"*Non sudare!*"—to avoid sweat.

In the piazza and on the beach, children are urged to slow down. Not because they might annoy those in the vicinity, but because they should not work up a dangerous sweat.

Sometimes the ambient temperature is so high that an Italian will break a sweat even while sitting in the shade. This is why they avoid air conditioning and carry a light sweater or scarf. If sweating is unavoidable then the dreaded draft must be evaded.

***Allora:*** Tourists may safely sweat in Italy, and they will.

# Italians Don't Jog

**Heard in Florence:** "Don't run, darling. You'll get all sweaty."

Maybe it is that Italian cities are full of uneven cobblestones or the fact that sweat pants and shorts are not considered proper attire for a city environment, but whatever the reason, Italians don't jog.

Most likely Italians don't jog because of the fear that sweat and exertion lead to overheating, which when mixed with the danger of the *colpo d'aria* (the dreaded draft), can lead to fatal consequences. Or maybe it's just that medieval cities don't have big parks with bike paths or jogging tracks. Medieval cities don't have sidewalks, either.

Italians will exert themselves for a good cause. During Florence's annual *Corri La Vita*, a race and walking event for breast cancer research, over 200,000 people turn out. The winners of the race are always foreigners, but plenty of Italians join in the run. Many more support the charity, get the t-shirt, and then go play "Italian Line" at the museums that are open free to participants wearing the *Corri La Vita* t-shirts.

There are marathons run in Rome and Florence, but those are for runners, not joggers, and the winners are predominately from some other country.

***Allora:*** An American out for her daily run will be alone in Italy. She may wish to avoid the perils of jogging on cobblestones by joining a gym. There she can run for miles in comfort.

# You Are What You Eat

**Heard in Florence:** "Don't put fresh milk in a full stomach."

Italians harbor grave concerns about the health of their internal organs and the result is a number of Food Rules:

Don't drink *cappuccino* or *caffelatte* after ten o'clock in the morning.

Don't put ice in beverages.

Don't drink citrus juice at dinner.

Don't snack.

Don't drink coffee during a meal.

Don't touch the fruits and vegetables in the market.

In a modern world full of food allergies and food phobias, however, Italians don't buy into the latest trending prohibitions in the U.S.. That may be due to the fact that they only eat Italian food cooked in Italy. Pasta-loving Italians do not talk about gluten-free diets,

251

but they also don't devour a loaf of bread from a basket on the table before a meal begins.

Italians equate good food with good health. They tend to eat dishes made of seasonal ingredients, grown locally. Therefore, the regional recipes are still the most popular. The citizens of the north only look to Sicily for citrus and wine. Seafood is consumed near the coast, rarely in the mountains.

Most Italians practice moderation in both food and drink. Obesity and alcoholism have traditionally not been health issues for Italians. Friends don't expect cocktails or even a glass of wine to be offered as soon as they arrive when invited to dinner in an Italian home. Wine is consumed in moderation, always with food.

Various sayings help keep things straight. The orange juice proverb warns: Orange in the morning is gold. Orange at lunch is silver. Orange at night is lead.

Italians talk a lot about perceived stomach and liver problems that they might be suffering. Those ailments will be attributed to the consumption of too much or too little of some ingredient in one of the meals eaten in the last 24 hours. The remedy will be the addition or deletion of some other ingredient, rarely a medicinal remedy, in the coming 24 hours.

***Allora:*** The Italian Food Rules are rich and varied. Most of them have a long history. Learn a few before you visit Italy. You will enjoy being Italian for a day, a week, or a month.

# DON'T DRINK THE WATER

**Heard in every restaurant in Italy:** "*Naturale o frizzante?*"

It took the bottled water industry a long time to start converting Americans to the "benefits" of their product. At home and while dining out, most people in the U.S. still drink only tap water, sometimes filtered, mostly not. Italians, on the other hand, lead Europeans per capita in bottled water consumption with an average of 150 liters (35 gallons) per person per year.

Whereas Americans and others are happy to have tap water, either refrigerated or iced, poured for them as soon as they sit down at a restaurant table, it is virtually impossible to get the same service in Italy. It is possible to be served tap water, but you must have sufficient Italian to make the request: "*Vorrei l'acqua del rubinetto, per favore.*" Once the request is made, the waiter may sneer at the choice. It is not because he wants to inflate the bill; he just would never consider drinking water from the tap himself. Furthermore, he may not

253

have a pitcher from which to serve tap water, necessitating carrying each glass to the table from the sink.

Although the water that comes out of the tap throughout Italy is perfectly potable, urban Italians drink almost exclusively bottled water that purportedly comes from "real" mountain springs and therefore, tastes better.

City tap water in many regions of Italy may have a strong chemical taste from the chlorine and other additives used to purify reservoir or well water. It can also taste very "hard" with high, but safe, concentrations of minerals such as calcium, sodium and potassium. Few Italians install water-softening systems in their homes, even though the white buildup of scale in shower stalls and hot water pots tells of high levels of calcium carbonate in the water.

Even in the Italian Alps, where the tap water is often piped, unprocessed, directly from mountain springs into homes, the residents drink bottled water with their meals. There is a subset of the mountain inhabitants – mostly elderly – who can be seen at roadside springs filling empty glass or plastic containers with fabulous tasting water from virtually the same source that the bottled water companies use.

Italian bottled water comes in a carbonated (*frizzante*) form and a non-carbonated (*naturale* or "no gas") variety. Most of the *frizzante* water has been artificially carbonated, but a few brands, such as Ferrarelle, are naturally fizzy. Italians are very loyal to the brand they feel "tastes the best." Everyone has an individual opinion about this.

Water is served with lunch and dinner. There seems to be an even split between those who drink carbonated water and those who prefer bottled still water. Often, especially during the summer, a splash of wine is added to water (usually carbonated) for a refreshing unsweetened drink.

The Brita-style water pitcher with a small filter is available in Italy, but has not become as popular as it is elsewhere. For home consumption, most city households buy bottled water in six packs of 1.5-liter bottles. With almost 300 different brands, about 12 billion liters, with an annual value of almost 2.5 billion euros, are produced in Italy each year. The average annual cost is about 400 euros for every Italian family.

San Pellegrino is a national brand known by most visitors. The water comes from near the town of San Pellegrino in the mountainous Dolomites of the north. The company is now owned by Nestle and its carbonated water is shipped all over the world.

In Rome someone has even opened a store dedicated to mineral water. There you can choose between 60 water brands coming from all over Europe and the U.S., even though in Rome there are more than 2,100 fountains providing very good drinking water for the citizens' use. Pliny the Elder (1st century BC) praised the "healthy waters" of Rome.

Not far from Rome, the spa town of Fiuggi produces a water known for its health-giving properties.

Reportedly, the waters cured Pope Boniface VIII (1235-1303) of a severe case of kidney stones. When word of the Pope's miraculous recovery spread among the ambassadors to the Vatican, casks of Fiuggi water were sent to all of Europe's reigning monarchs. Michelangelo also suffered from kidney stones ("the only kind of stone I couldn't love," he reportedly said) until he became a habitual drinker of Fiuggi water.

As the Italian environmental consciousness deepens and the cost of dealing with plastic waste rises, mayors throughout the peninsula are starting to promote what was previously unthinkable: that Italians should drink tap water.

In Venice, trash is an especially costly problem because men must collect it with wheelbarrows, push it to the side of the canals, and then ship it out via barges. Collection costs $335 per ton compared with $84 per ton on the mainland. City officials, copying the marketing that has helped make bottled water a multibillion-dollar global industry, invented a lofty brand name for Venice's tap water, Acqua Veritas, and created a sleek logo emblazoned on stylish carafes that were distributed free to households. They have made sure everyone now knows: Venice's tap water comes from deep underground in the same region as the popular bottled water, San Benedetto. In terms of trash reduction, the Acqua Veritas campaign has already been a success, Venetian officials calculate, reducing the amount of plastic trash by 25 tons a month. Italy's most loyal buyers of bottled water live in Tuscany. So Florence's water

utility, Publiacqua, has tried to re-brand it:
uct. Publiacqua's new fountains, most pro
the west side of the Palazzo Vecchio, pro
tines with ultra-filtered water for free. The fountains
can deliver about 80 gallons of water an hour and have
an internal computer that monitors water quality and
output. For the first time, the city is offering public water without a chlorine or mineral aftertaste.

The Florentines call this "the mayor's water" (*acqua del sindaco*). The taps produce both still and carbonated water. Although there are long lines of
tourists at the free water spigots in the summer, the
program has made little headway with restaurants and
stores, which make money selling bottled water. And in
a city where tourists outnumber permanent residents
100 to 1, public education that concentrates on locals
can go only so far in reducing plastic waste. If Florentines do choose to stand in line to fill up their own bottles, the habit could begin to chip away at the bottled
water industry.

***Allora:*** Tourists may wish to utilize the free refill
of water bottles offered by certain Italian communities
and can safely drink the water at their hotel or rental
apartment, but for the most part must resign themselves to purchasing expensive bottled water when dining out.

# PANACEA FOR EVERYTHING

**Heard in Viterbo:** "Quit crying. Now that the bleeding has stopped, I'm going to put some propolis on your knee."

My mother thought that A&D Ointment and Vick's VapoRub could cure just about anything from a cut or bruise to pneumonia to a scratch on the coffee table. In Italy, mothers make the same claims about olive oil and propolis.

Most everyone around the world knows about the properties of olive oil, but propolis is less well known outside of Italy. Propolis is a resin that bees collect from plants and tree sap, and is used to do the following: reinforce the structural stability of the hive; reduce vibration; make the hive more defensible by sealing alternate entrances; prevent diseases and parasites from entering the hive; to inhibit fungal and bacterial growth; and prevent putrefaction within the hive. It has approximately 50 constituents, primarily resins and vegetable balsams (50 percent), waxes (30 percent), essential and aromatic oils (10 percent), and pollen (5 percent).

Since ancient Roman times, propolis has also been incorporated into numerous medical and cosmetic products since it is believed to be a potent antiseptic and anti-inflammatory substance, local anesthetic, astringent, and antioxidant. Italian mothers know that propolis also: has an antimicrobial, antibacterial and antifungal activity; is an emollient for treating the inflammatory component of skin burns; is an immuno-modulator, immunosuppressive and immuno-stimulant; is a treatment for allergies (except for those allergic to bee sting); is an oral hygiene product, preventing cavities and canker sores; is an antioxidant; and is effective in cancer treatment and cancer prevention.

Like my mother's use of A&D ointment, an Italian house wife will use propolis as a furniture polish, and it is used by most stringed instrument makers in Cremona to enhance the appearance of the wood grain of violins, violas, and cellos. It is a component of some varnishes and its distinctive smell is easily recognizable in a *liutaio's* shop. Antonio Stradivari and his colleagues undoubtedly used propolis in the early 18th century.

Propolis freshens breath and thus is used by some chewing gum manufacturers to make propolis gum, but it can also be used to bring about a chemical reaction to convert fats and oils into automobile wax during application to a Ferrari or a Fiat 500.

In Italy, swallow a spoonful of olive oil and rub on some propolis and all will go right with the world.

***Allora:*** Propolis and olive oil are easy to find in

Italy. Take some back to your country and you may find they are the cure for what ails you.

# THE ANARCHY OF SHUTTERS

**Heard in Florence:** "Anarchy," said my Florentine friend, "I like it."

"What are you talking about?" I asked.

"Look up there," she said, pointing to the top floor of a medieval building in the center of Florence.

"I don't see anything anarchical."

"The shutters. They are turquoise." She pointed at a pair of small shutters on one window on the top floor where a noble family's servants once lived.

Sure enough, they were a light blue-green — different from every other shutter in Florence. They were also absolutely illegal under the code of the *Belle Arti*, the governing body that regulates all aspects of historical buildings in Florence. All buildings in the center of the city are deemed to be historical.

Shutters in Florence and Tuscany, as well as some other regions in Italy, can only be dark brown, black, dark gray or dark green. Any other hue or lighter shade of one of the allowed colors is deemed out of compliance. The owner can expect a registered letter in the mail demanding change on threat of a substantial fine.

Shutters are important to the smooth running of Italian life. Not the color, just the use of shutters. Only Americans and the British throw open their shutters and windows on a sweltering summer day in hopes of catching a stray breeze. (As in "mad dogs and English-men go out in the mid-day sun." Noel Coward) The Italians know that windows and shutters must be closed by nine in the morning to hold in the night's coolness and then at sunset they must be opened throughout the house to *cambiare l'aria* (change the air) throughout the night. Of course, the window in the bedroom will be closed as the occupants retire to pre-vent the dreaded draft (*colpo d'aria*) from striking the exposed necks or tummies of unwary sleepers. In the morning the process starts again.

The other kind of window shutter, the heavy roll-ing wood or metal blind, known as a *avvolgibile* or *tap-parella,* is found on most modern buildings (less than 100-years old) and provide the same service for stand-ardized windows. (They are also better at denying entry to cat burglars.)

The lack of standardized windows make tradi-tional wooden shutters a more common sight in the historical cities of Italy, but also prevents the use of screens to deny entry of the ever-present mosquitos.

***Allora:*** If a visitor to Italy becomes so enchanted that life under the Tuscan sun is the only answer, they must remember that there is a rule or permit that will govern almost every aspect of their renovation project.

# BAN WALL-TO-WALL CARPETS

**Heard in Matera:** "Why would your British wife want to carpet the bedroom? Doesn't she know what hides in carpets?"

It used to be that British and the French perpetuated the myth that the Italians were peasants, living in filth. Read books and essays published in the early 20th century and after WWII in England. Listen to the French as they cross the border in Liguria.

Nothing could be further from the truth. Wall-to-wall carpets prove it.

Remember the shag carpets so popular in the 60s and 70s throughout Britain and the U.S.? Even now, most American and European homes have carpet in the bedrooms and living rooms. But not all Continental countries are tacking that thick wool shag or durable smooth sisal weave into the corners. The Swiss rank first in their disdain for wall-to-wall carpets. The Italians run a close second.

Few Italian families tolerate wall-to-wall carpeting. With a rug that cannot be taken out, hung on a line and beaten clean, there is no control of the dirt clinging to the fibers or weave. Not even the strongest vacuum cleaner, used every single day, can assure the Italian homemaker that what is lurking deep in the pile of a carpet has been sucked away.

The Germans argue the opposite, holding that allowing the carpet to cling to dust and spores lessens allergic symptoms. Italians declare that it is much better to have floors that can be swept every day and mopped with hot soapy water every other day. To some, small washable throw rugs or shakable area carpets are acceptable to break up the cold and noise of tile, marble and terra cotta floors.

In England and France, you will not see the lady of the house wash down the front stoop every day, or store owners washing the sidewalk and street in front of the shop door, but you will observe the practice in every Italian town. It's true that Italians are litterers and frequently fail to clean up after their dogs; this infuriates the Americans and the British. Outside a radius of a couple of meters from their street door, Italians know that the world is a filthy place and there is nothing much they can do about it. In the Italian home, however, with a ban on outside shoes, the use of *pantofole* (slippers) and no wall-to-wall carpets, the environment is dust- and germ-free.

***Allora:*** When entering an Italian home, don't be surprised if your host or hostess is wearing slippers. If you are comfortable doing so, ask if she would prefer for you to remove your shoes.

# AIR CONDITIONING CAN KILL YOU

**Heard at a hotel in Como:** "I know it's unseasonably hot for June, but our air conditioning is not turned on until July."

The visitor to Italy never knows how much they liked air conditioning until it was gone. When it is hot Americans in the U.S. go from an air conditioned home to an air conditioned car to an air conditioned office or supermarket or mall.

June can be hot in Italy, but then there is July and August when the weather gets switched from "bake" to "broil," and the temperature is in the 90s or above every day and it's humid. At night, the ancient stones hold in the heat and so it doesn't cool down that much. But to find a hotel or apartment with air conditioning is sometimes difficult.

Unless the building was built after 1970, rare in Italy, it is unlikely to have central air conditioning. To install AC in medieval buildings requires tunneling through stone walls to insert the tubes from the unit on the roof. Non-standard windows cannot hold an AC unit and the zoning laws written to maintain the look of the Renaissance throughout the country forbid hanging modern contraptions on the outside walls. The portable unit, known as a *pinguino* for obvious reasons, is noisy and requires venting through a porthole in the window.

The most important consideration, however, is that Italians don't really believe in air conditioning. They think that cold air on your body makes you sick. They are even suspicious of fans. This is, of course, the problem of *colpo d'aria* – that dreaded draft; the cold air on your neck giving you neck pain and of course, making you sick.

There is not even a reprieve in going for a long drive in the car because, of course, many Italians don't have AC installed in their cars, or if it is installed, they don't use it. Opening the car window may lead to a debate of whether the *colpo d'aria* (blast of air) is dangerous to exposed sweat-covered skin.

**Allora:** The tourist in a restaurant or store or on a bus will never win the argument that the air conditioning should be turned up. In July and August, make an advance trip before booking a restaurant or inquire before making hotel reservations to assure that the temperature is to your liking.

# HUNG OUT TO DRY

**Heard in Florence:** "It's not going to rain. Hang those sheets outside the window … well, maybe cover them with a bit of plastic."

Much of the year Florence has the worst air quality of any city in Italy, but that does not stop Florentines from hanging their laundry outside. Just run a finger over the bookshelves in your Florence apartment and you will find an oily gray residue, even though you dusted yesterday. It's a combination of car, bus and scooter exhaust and the dust of 1,000-year old buildings crumbling. Florentines worry about what the air is doing to their lungs, but they will argue to the end that hanging clothes in the "fresh" air is the only way to dry everything from sheets and towels to blue jeans and intimate undies.

Ancient Italian apartment buildings are not wired with sufficient voltage to power a traditional clothes dryer. (Remember when you shorted out the electricity of the entire hotel when you plugged in your hair dryer?) Also, electricity in Italy is too expensive to waste it on drying clothes. Finally, Italians take the most righteous position and claim they just want to save the planet one load of laundry at a time.

Americans have clothes dryers that look like small alien spaceships with enough dials and lights to dry a dozen types of fabric to an equal number of levels of dampness or dryness, including the ever-popular "cool air fluff" cycle that goes on and on to avoid wrinkles. Italians would rather fire up the steam iron to finish off those sheets and tablecloths.

The French find the lines of drying clothes hanging from window to window in Italy to be untidy, the sign of slovenliness. Italians use whites, darks and pastels pinned to ropes on pulleys across the streets in Naples as a way to check on the laundry skills of the housewife next door as well as an excuse to catch up on the neighborhood gossip while hanging the wash.

Small eco-friendly dryers and neighborhood coin-operated laundromats with mammoth dryers have come to Italy so the prevalence of laundry flapping in the breeze may someday become a thing of the past, but not as long as the generation of "fresh air" advocates have their say.

***Allora:*** When packing for a month in Italy, the choice of easy wash and wear clothing will make a long-stay visitor's life simpler and without wrinkles.

# TINY BOXES

**Heard in an elevator in Verona:** "Why won't it go. We only have three people in here."

Supposedly, Italy has greater elevator density for its population than any other country in the world. That would be great news for the traveler with suitcases, but the fact that Italians like to live together in two to four story buildings rather than single family dwelling brings the statistic into sharper focus. In a city like Florence almost everyone lives in a building that has at least four stories and the apartments start on the second floor. Only 10 percent of the buildings in Florence have elevators. Visitors should keep this in mind when selecting hotels and packing that extra suitcase.

When the historical zoning commissions try to maintain the Renaissance ambience of Florence, elevators don't fit into the equation. Then try to get a condominium association for a building with ten apartments to agree to pay for the installation of an elevator into their 500-year old building, especially those living on the first two floors. Installation of a tiny elevator usually requires the cutting away of half of the width of the ancient *pietra serena* stone that makes up the stairway. In many of the narrower buildings, such stairway surgery is impossible given the width of the stairway.

The government realizes that access issues for an aging population require some action, so laws have been passed mandating that buildings with two stairways must install an elevator. Since not more than 20 percent of the existing buildings have two stairways the effect will not be great.

Slowly, slowly, some train stations are getting elevators to ease the accessibility to the tracks, but they are usually impossible to locate or out of order and the trains still don't have automated lifts into the cars and the doors don't open even with the platform so the access added by the few elevators this is still largely for naught.

***Allora:*** Never try to overcrowd an Italian elevator. If the sign says three people is the maximum capacity, believe it.

# WHAT ITALIANS DO IN BED

**Heard in Milan:** "*Tesoro*, get that pen away from my Frette sheets."

The following activities are permissible in an Italian's bed: sleeping, watching television, sex, texting or telephoning, and, perhaps, reading (books, not newspapers (too much noise)).

The following activities are not allowed: eating or drinking, working (documents, pens, pencils, or computers), filling or emptying suitcases and gym bags, napping and pet activities.

The allowable activities are self-explanatory. The foreigner may have trouble understanding the prohibitions, except for the eating and drinking one. Italians know that eating and drinking in bed leads to crumbs and stains. Also, there are a whole raft of food rules that pertain to the proper time and place to eat.

Pens and pencils raise the same stain and grit factor. Documents are meant to be managed at a desk and computers are noisy and distracting and rarely offer activities to bed partners, and so lead to altercations. Suit-cases and gym bags have had contact with surfaces outside the house and thus should never touch bedcovers or bed linens.

Napping, unless accompanied by complete disrobing and/or pajamas, is to be done on a chair or couch. Pets do not wear shoes and so their bare paws have had contact with the floor leading to dust and pathogens on the bed linens, without the mention of hair, dander and saliva.

***Allora:*** The following items are bad luck when placed on an Italian's bed: money, hairbrushes, and hats. Shoes on the bed (either being worn or not) are just disgusting and shouldn't be allowed in any society.

# TO BIDET OR NOT TO BIDET

**Heard in a hotel in Perugia:** "Mom, there's a toilet for toddlers in this bathroom!"

Americans often wonder about the extra item found in many Italian bathrooms. It looks like a hybrid between a sink and a toilet, but it is not either. It is the bidet. Italians love their bidets and think Americans and the Brits are coarse, uncouth and dirty creatures for not using them. Americans can barely look at a bidet without laughing. The British just find them embarrassing to think about.

Bidets were an 18th century French invention, and the word bidet actually comes from the old French "to trot" or "pony." This is because the bidet user is said to look like someone riding a pony. Bidets must have made a lot of sense back then. There was no indoor plumbing and thus, no showers and to fill the bathtub with hot water was hard work. In modern times, the number of Italian bidets exceeds those used by the French.

Many people around the world wrongly think that

Italians might lack personal hygiene because they'd prefer a quick rinse in the nether regions to a proper shower. False. The accepted philosophy is that you shower, on average, once daily and use the bidet two or three times "as needed." Even the smallest bathroom in an Italian home will have a bidet, even if it has to forego the walled shower stall.

Some say that the bidet was adopted in Italy for the *siesta-tresca*. Until recently, Italians took a long afternoon siesta. Stores would close down from one to five and schools would let out at one for the day. Families would meet at home to eat together and take a rest. "*Tresca*" is an Italian word meaning "little fling" or "love affair". Back in the 60s or 70s Italian men would have lunch with their family then maybe stop in to see their lover for the *siesta-tresca* before going back to work. The bidet was used for a quick wash-up after the *siesta-tresca*.

A bidet can be useful for so many things, besides the obvious. It makes a great baby bath. Lots of visitors to Italy use it to wash their tired feet. You can rinse out dirty baby clothes in it, or hand-wash your own. Only American and Aussie men think it is a great place to ice down beer. Italians refuse to use the bidet for anything other than its original intimate purpose.

***Allora:*** Once a visitor to Italy learns the benefits of a bidet and the proper method of use, she may considered getting one installed back home. Many have.

# ITALIAN FOOD, ONLY ITALIAN FOOD

**Heard in Brooklyn:** "You call this Italian food? My mother doesn't make it this way."

Italians love Italian food. This seems self-evident, but let's go a step further. Italians love Italian food, only Italian food.

This explains why it is virtually impossible to find a restaurant in Italy serving Thai food, or Indian food, or French food. Someone will, of course, raise the point that, unlike the U.S. or Britain, Italy does not have sufficient immigrants from Thailand, India or France to provide a basis for these eateries. But Italy does have large Filipino, African, Peruvian, and Eastern European immigrant groups and there are no restaurants serving food from the Philippines, Africa, Peru or the Ukraine. This is because Italians only eat Italian food.

In Florence there is one Mexican restaurant (the chef is German), three or four hamburger joints, a half dozen Chinese restaurants and a couple of sushi bars.

Who eats at these places? American students, Chinese and Japanese tour groups, and very few adventuresome, mostly young, Italians.

In all of the international surveys, people throughout the world rate Italian food as their favorite cuisine, followed by Chinese. Italians are correct in their love of their own recipes. The ingredients are sourced locally, the dishes are cooked up within minutes of the order, and the recipes have been tested over centuries.

When Italians travel, they might try the food of other countries, but for the most part this leads to dissatisfaction, which results in the search for a place that serves Italian food. Luckily for Italians, it is hard to find a tourist destination throughout the world that does not have an Italian restaurant. Even countries with no history of Italian emigration—Japan, China, Mexico, Iceland—there are Italian restaurants.

Italians on vacation, however, are more disappointed with the Italian food they find in other countries than they are with the local traditional cuisine. The pasta will be deemed inferior, the sauces are canned, the fresh ingredients are not the same as those available back home, the spicing is all wrong. They return to Italy praising the fabulous shopping, the great sales, the friendly customer service, the incredible museums, the awe-inspiring skyscrapers, the vast national parks, the comfy hotel rooms and, at the same time, bemoaning the horrible food.

Even Luca Parmitano, an Italian astronaut,

planned ahead for his six-month stay on the international space station. On a payload that went up before his flight he made sure that *pesto risotto*, *lasagna*, *melanzane alla parmigiana*, *mushroom risotto*, and *tiramisu* were included. These Italian specialties might not have been as good as Luca's mother makes them, since they had to be vacuum-packed, but at least he won't be eating Russian borscht or American beef jerky. The questions remain if Luca will share his *cibo buono* with his international colleagues and whether he will be able to pair a nice Chianti Classico with the mushroom *risotto*.

*__Allora:__* When in Italy give up the idea of eating any other type of cuisine. You will thank yourself, as the Italians do when they find a compatriot has started a restaurant with *cibo vero*, true food, in Chicago.

# SAME BEACH, SAME SEA

**Heard on the beach at Viareggio:** "Get out of the water, Gino. It's not 10am yet."

Only death or divorce will get you a spot in the coveted first row on an Italian beach. In a country where there is a socialistic equality in most things – health care, long lines at the post office, job security, good food – the beach is not one of them. In the U.S., if you get up early enough, you can stake out the best piece of sand on almost any shore and you can usually have a couple of yards between you and your nearest neighbor.

In Italy, the best spot is already taken – everywhere. This prime real estate is a ten-foot square piece of sand on the front row (closest to the waterline) in one of the hundreds of beach stations (*stabilimenti balneari* or *bagni*) that line the sandy beach along the gently rolling Tyrrhenian Sea from Rome to Cinque Terre. It is only obtained through patience or primogeniture.

This, of course, is not the natural sea-washed, wind-ruffled, damp towel-covered, littered, beer

281

cooler- and shell-strewn beach of the U.S. or Britain. No, this is ten feet of perfectly groomed sand, topped by a large beach umbrella, a beach chair, two matching sling-back chairs and a long lounge with attached sun-shade.

It is crowded, especially after the allowable five people move into the space. It's more crowded when the neighboring *ombrelloni* (beach umbrellas) on either side are raised and their quota of five people each arrive. But, of course, if you have a spot on the front row, you know everyone around you – they have been friends, or even family, for decades.

Each summer Italians spend as much time as possible, not only in the same seaside town, or at the same *bagno*, but also on the same spot of sand, the same distance from the same sea. They frequently rent the spot for three to four months each year. When no member of the extended family is present between the months of May to mid-September, no one else is allowed to sit under their umbrella, on their chairs, or on their small plot of sand.

For Americans who for the most part don't spend the summer holidays in the same place twice, this shows an astonishing commitment or a sad lack of imagination. But this is not unusual for Italians. A recent study showed that over 70 percent of Italians take their 30 to 60 days of vacation each summer at the same time and over 65 percent spend that holiday time in the exact same place every year.

Perhaps it is the chaos of their history and politics

that push Italians into a comfortable conformity in their private lives. They have a sense of humor about it all. In the 1960s, Piero Focaccia, a popular singer, warbled this tune:

*Per quest'anno, non cambiare.*
*Stessa spiaggia, stesso mare.*

For this year, don't change
Same beach, same sea.

Italy is blessed with beaches, both east on the Adriatic Sea or west on the adjoining seas: Ligurian, Tyrrhenian, as well as the southern Ionian Sea. The personalities of the coasts are clearly defined. The east coast has thousands of *stabilimenti* lined up at Rimini, Ancona, San Benedetto and Lido di Jesolo, south to Pescara. The sea is flat and tepid, but the beaches rock with discos and luna parks. The west coast has more rambunctious seas, but seems to have a more placid beach life, fewer teenagers looking to hook up, more groups of three or four middle-aged ladies standing knee-deep in the water gossiping. Italians are opinionated and loyal – those that favor the east coast, do not let the west coast sand slide between their toes.

Actually, there is not a lot of sand-toe contact on the Italian beaches. Once the Italian family (this is not a solitary pastime; you only go to the beach with family or friends) selects its preferred coast, picks a town to match their socio-economic class (Forte dei Marmi for high-rollers, Viareggio and Lido di Camaiore for the well-to-do, Marina di Massa Carrara for the middle class) and puts down one to five thousand euro for the 16 summer weeks (mid-May to mid September) at a bath station.

For the American with an exaggerated sense of personal space, the Italian beach scene, although colorful, can seem claustrophobic. For the Italian it is a joyful place of friends and family – teenagers fall in love, get married ten years later, socialize and play cards with other couples, have children, who played together as babies/toddlers/teenagers, and then fall in love and start the cycle all over again.

As the summer ends and the *ombrelloni* are put away, Italians say goodbye to their beach-mates with promises of "*stessa spiaggia, stesso mare*" next year.

***Allora:*** Every visitor to Italy, who arrives in July or August, should go the beach to observe the Italians in their summer habitat, but don't think that you will get an umbrella on the front row.

# BEACH LIFE ITALIAN STYLE

**Heard on the beach at Forte dei Marmi:** "Did you see Barbara flirting with the *bagnino* last night?"

Nowhere else can you observe the Italian national character in all its exaggerated glory than every August at the beach. Since the Italian coast is almost all beach, except for a bit at Cinque Terre and a section of the Amalfi, you have a lot of opportunities.

Your first sight will invoke the Italian sense of color and design with line upon line of identically-colored beach umbrellas and deck chairs (two full-length lounge beds and three small deck chairs for each umbrella) stretching away left and right as far as the eye could see. Every hundred yards or so the color scheme of the *ombrelloni* and furniture will change. A shot from a spy satellite in June must give the sense of an over-the-top rainbow-colored Dolce & Gabbana thigh-high boot glittering against the Mediterranean blue.

Next you will be drowned in Italian family dynamics. To get the full experience the time to arrive is June or early July. For two months the weather is only an oven set for baking bread. In August, the broiler gets turned on. For the first two summer months, young mothers and old grandmothers and the single only child/grandchild will populate the beach. (Since WWII, one-child families have been the norm so now the third generation is scampering on the beach in search of a friend). Over fifty percent of Italian women do not work outside the home, so they are at the beach by June. Working fathers appear on the weekends only before August. (Extra-marital affairs spike in June and July for both men (in town) and women (beachside).)

There is not a lot of lazing in bed for mother and child. *Nonna*, the grandmother, will mandate that the sun is best between seven and nine and that they should be walking slowly along the water's edge, breathing deeply to give the child's lungs the benefit of the fresh clean morning air. The child cannot actually enter the water, of course. The sea will not be warm enough for feet or ankles before 10am. Therefore, until the appointed hour everyone walks up and down the beach, an activity known as the *passeggiata*. (The stroll will take place again in the evening before six.) No running is allowed for the children, though. Excessive activity of any kind is frowned upon as unhealthy and irritating. (No adult will be jogging on the beach, either.)

After the morning *passeggiata,* but before settling at their designated *ombrelloni,* mother and grandmother will stop for a cappuccino and pastry (the child would have had bread with Nutella and a glass of milk before starting out from their vacation apartment) from the *barista* at their bathing station's *café*.

Beside the *barista* the most important person to ensure a successful day at the beach is the *bagnino*, the lifeguard. He will occasionally run his red boat into the waves to drag out a sputtering child, but more importantly he is responsible for the manicured sand and the precise set-up of the *ombrelloni* and chairs, as well as the arbiter of which persons have paid for the right to a place near or far from the sea. At the slightest sign of bad weather—when a breeze twitching the tassels on the *ombrelloni*—the red flag will go up and the *bagnino* will warn you to stay out of the water. He is not obligated to save anyone who ignores the warning. He is the keeper of all gossip, and the go-to guy for a summer fling. For the voyeur, observing the daily life of the *bagnino* is most gratifying.

Italian fashion culture is also displayed at the beach. For example, children will have at least three to four changes of clothes during the day. There will be the morning walk outfit, including beach shoes—no bare feet before 10am. When the water is warm enough, a swimming suit will be exposed. After the morning plunge there is the mandatory rinse at the beachside showers, followed by the cocooning in a hooded robe. Before lunch there may be another shower, thorough drying and a new outfit. After the afternoon *riposo* (the obligatory three-hour rest between food and returning to the sea, a different swim-suit will be used (the morning one may still be damp). At the end of the day, a sweater or windbreaker will be added to the outfit for the evening *passeggiata* to ward off the evening breezes. Finally, a set of clothes will be selected for dinner at a pizzeria or fish restaurant. Adults will have at least as many fashion decisions throughout the day.

Where are the teenagers, you ask. They are invariably out late so they make an appearance at the family *ombrelloni* around noon. They'll cadge some coins for lunch and then join their friends. Summer holidays are famous for being an occasion for the first quasi-sexual experience. Teenagers hardly ever enter the water, not wanting to ruin the look that took hours and half a tube of gel to perfect (and that's just the boys). They gather in same-sex groups, the girls at the tables with their smartphones, the boys round the nearby video games, but eyeing each other. The beach-volleyball court provided by the beach station gets a lot of action each day. It's a subtle way to show off new bikinis, suntans, and muscle definition.

At the Italian beach where the same people at the same place surround you every day, year after year, the surprises get fewer and fewer every year. You know who is a morning person; what music they are listening to through their earbuds (no loud music allowed); what they look like topless and if they've been augmented (though for ladies, only lying down topless; walking topless is not allowed), if they read, what they read;

what soccer team they support; whether they snack or have an eating disorder; if they are pregnant, getting a divorce, or having an affair; if they are bringing their children up "right" (a kid building a sandcastle has clearly not been told by his mother that this is not allowed); any recent surgeries; who misses their dog (pets are not allowed); if their politics are liberal or conservative; how their parents are aging; and on and on.

The beach is also for shopping. First, a man from Morocco or Tunisia comes by with a sloshing bucket of coconut pieces in water. A tall Somalian trudges through the sand with 20 colorful beach towels over his shoulder, as well as cotton pants and scarves made in his country. Out on the boardwalk, until 1pm and throughout the evening, stores sell Prada sandals, Borsalino Panama hats, Gucci bags and sexy La Perla swimwear for the ladies or the French Vilebrequin swim trunks (120 euro per pair) with solid gold aglets for the man who want just a little bling.

The rest of the world may worry about an epidemic of melanoma and slather on the SPF 50 sunscreen lotion, but Italians are worried about appearing unwell and pallid. During the winter, tanning beds are very popular. During the summer, the beach, a lounge bed, a Speedo or a string bikini are all the protection needed from the sun's rays.

"But isn't there a beach public," you ask. Yes, in every town, on every seafront, there's an empty space that measures about 100 square yards. The sand, what there is of it, is not raked—it is a lumpy mess of sandy rocks, rotting seaweed, and twisted driftwood. A couple of dogs sniff about (dogs are allowed) a single, small beach umbrella jammed into the sand shades the picnic of a heavy-set guy, wearing swimming trunks, black socks and sandals and a woman with a radiant sunburn and a string bikini. It's the public beach. Every town has to leave one spot of beach free for those who won't or can't pay. The picnicking couple is from Germany and down the way on a big towel is a family from Canada. The eight-year old child has built a five-foot sandcastle (sandcastles are allowed). Three teenage boys are kicking a soccer ball while listening to Italian rap on the radio. They are locals from town. (Games and music are allowed on the public beach.)

Looking at these *tristi* tourists "roughing it" shows how the "private" Italian beach experience is an illusion—the beautifully raked white sand, the colorful *ombrelloni*, the socialization, fabulous food, regulations, the *barista* and the *bagnino*. It's the Italian character distilled—not too risky, comfortable, family-centric, on show for all to see, in close quarters, with plenty of *pesci fritti* (fried fish), pasta and pizza.

**Allora:** To really understand the Italian personality, a long-term visitor to Italy must rent an *ombrellone* for a week and participate in Italian beach life.

# EMPTY INFERNO

**Heard all over Italy:** "Where did everybody go?"

*Ferragosto*, the 15th of August, the day that the Holy Mother Mary ascended into heaven, would seem to be the most important holiday to Italians. It is the day that 100 percent of the country seems to get into a vehicle and head somewhere—beach, mountains, fishing—only to find themselves in a nation-wide traffic jam. This only seems strange when one realizes that about 80 percent of the country is already on vacation. August is the month when Italian factories, restaurants, movie theaters, shops, even *gelaterias* (except for those in the vacation meccas on the coast or in the mountains) close for four weeks of vacation.

A frustrated foreign expat has said, "It is culturally inappropriate to get your needs met before September." She meant that if you happen to be one of the handful of people sweltering at home in Rome or Florence during August and your hot water heater conks out, you will be taking cold showers until September when the plumbers return, tanned and rested, to the city. The same is true for an electrical glitch, a chipped tooth, a broken bicycle chain, the package from Australia you are expecting, or the prescription you forgot to renew in July.

It used to be more economical for Italian businesses to let everyone vacation at once, turning off the costly electrical lights and air-conditioning, parking the gas-guzzling delivery trucks, and saving time and money in a month when nothing gets done anyway. Once multi-national companies started to creep onto the scene, this became more difficult, but Italians still fought for the time off. Families had multi-generational histories of being at the same *bagno*, under the same *ombrellone* on the same beach in front of the same sea every August.

Italians live very well within the system. They plan to see doctors or dentists in July or schedule the yearly visit in July for September. They know that unless you live in a scenic mountain town or a lively beach enclave that only the state-run museums, the post office, large supermarkets, and a smattering of banks will be open during August. They know that they must see a popular movie in July, it won't show in August and it will be gone in September. Favorite TV shows will go on hiatus in August; it's time to watch a DVD or two, rented in July, of course.

The local TV news will be abbreviated in August, but all of the channels will show the same footage on August 1st, August 15th, and August 31st—the migration of Italians bumper to bumper to and from *le va-canze*.

Of course there are those perverse individuals who extoll the pleasures of Florence or Rome "when all those Italians are gone." But just wait until their pocket is picked and they find that the local police station is closed for a week of *ferie*.

**Allora:** August is the month to go to the museums. These institutions are guaranteed to be open. Although the city, state and regional museums may be crowded with visitors from all parts of the world, they will not be full of Italians.

# At Home at the Campground

**Heard at a campground in the Maremma:** "Our satellite TV is down. Are you getting a signal?"

In the U.S. the concept of "going camping" includes a tent, a campfire, hamburgers, instant coffee, water, a couple changes of clothes, sport shoes or hiking boots, sunscreen and trail mix. In Italy, going camping is much like going to the beach. Italians who "camp" go to the same campground and the same campsite at the same time, every year. They may have a trailer, an RV or a tent, but they will also have a pasta pot and a *caffettiera* (moka pot), a radio, a TV, a camp stove or, in the case of a trailer or RV, a kitchen stove, a full set of pasta bowls, plates, glasses and silverware, a bicycle or two, a case of red wine and another of *acqua frizzante*, cell phones and iPads, a folding table with sufficient folding chairs for each member of the family, an awning or large umbrella, indoor and outdoor footwear, bathrobes, disco clothes, beachwear, and, I kid you not, a washing machine and a dishwasher.

Some of the enormous family tents have several

rooms and high-tech accessories. Tent envy has been known to occur. It's as if the condominium of the towns and cities have been moved outdoors and some of the walls have come down. Now instead of just hearing your neighbors' lives, you can watch them, too.

An American family may be camping in an organized campground in a national park that might provide picnic tables and bathrooms, or, out in the wild with no extra facilities. The point is to get back to nature. An Italian family will be at a *villaggi* where there will be bathrooms and showers, a swimming pool, a beach if it is at the seaside, a coffee bar, a pizzeria, a game center equipped with electronic games, pinball and foosball tables, an outdoor movie theater, a *gelateria*, a general store, a newsstand, tennis and bocce ball courts, mini golf, and laundry facilities. The point is to get out of town.

The *animazione* games are organized by an *'equipe'* team of enthusiastic young people or drama students who run around among tents, caravans, mobile homes and bungalows trying to persuade people to join in. They arrange playgroups for children of different ages, sketches, competitions, karaoke, limbo dances, discos and outings.

"Glamping"—a fusion of glamour and camping—is now an international phenomenon, but the Italians have been doing this forever. Both independent properties and global hospitality brands have capitalized on an exploding demand of travelers who want to experience the positive aspects of camping without the "uncomfortable" negatives.

Some of the Italian campsites are located on prime real estate. In Florence, in an olive grove right next to Piazza Michelangelo with a panoramic view of the city is a campground called Camping Michelangelo. Near Verona, the campground is rewarded with the best view of the city made famous by the love story of Romeo and Juliet. The campsite near Siena, amid tall cypress trees, has an authentic taste of the Tuscan countryside – like living in a villa in the heart of Tuscany without the cost of renting a villa. In Cinque Terre the campsite is a steep hike away from the port, but is located in a quiet, fragrant lemon grove with yet another unbeatable view.

Near Milan, however, the campsite, Camping Village Città di Milano, is next to the parking lot of a Luna Park. Sheep, chickens and goats released from the park's petting zoo, reportedly patrol the campground at night. In Venice, the mosquito-filled campsite, Camping Village Jolly, is located in the industrial suburb of Marghera. It has all of the amenities of the Italian campgrounds, but includes bus service to the Grand Canal.

The most popular campgrounds are located at the seaside, operating from May through September and are like little temporary villages. The map legend for Plus Camping Roma is intricate and provides a grocery store, a swimming pool, a bar, an outdoor cinema and a night club, laundry facilities, free Internet and shuttle buses straight to St. Peter's Square. In the afternoon, the P.A. system blares the name of the movie shown later by the pool, as well as the bar's happy hour drink special. At the bar it is possible to get free Wi-Fi and write that e-mail or Skype with your mother who will be joining you next week.

Camping in Italy is not about getting away from others; it is just about getting away from home, but everywhere Italians go they carry with them the contents and culture of their homes.

***Allora:*** Camping in Italy is rarely fun for anyone who is not Italian, unless they happen to be German.

# Shoes Italian Style

**Heard in an apartment in Como:** "Are those the shoes you wore outside today? Take them off now. Put on your slippers."

Italy is famous for its shoes and rightly so. There are, however, rules about which pair of shoes is appropriate for each occasion and location.

The short and unchanging list: shoes and sandals for town wear (be it a village or city); sports shoes for participating in sporting events; flip-flops or rubber sandals for the beach or poolside; shower shoes for public or hotel showers; and slippers for home.

The trend-setting Italians base their choice of shoe both on reasons of style and of health.

The sidewalks, streets, and floors in the world outside the home are not controlled or cleaned by the Italian mother, or by anyone trained to clean by the Italian mother. Thus, all surfaces outside the home are suspect and assumed to contain large amounts of deadly pathogens. Shoes and sandals, depending on the weather, are to be worn at all times when outside the home, except when participating in a sport or at the beach.

No professional Italian woman transits (on foot, via car, scooter or bicycle, or on public transportation) to work wearing sports shoes with her designer slacks or skirt. Sports shoes are to be worn when participating in sporting events. Men may be let off the hook if they are wearing designer sporting shoes with casual attire.

Italian women (and Italian transvestites) have an innate talent for walking in stilettos. No matter what the surface—cobblestone, grass, pavement, marble—they glide along without stumbling, tripping, twisting an ankle, falling or even looking silly.

Italian women can also ride a scooter or a bicycle while wearing stilettos. Italian doctors warn about the dangers of the Italian footwear, but Italian women know better.

The term "stiletto" is a diminutive of the Italian *stilo*, which means "dagger." This term is derived from the Latin *stilus*, or "spike." Stilettos were widely used in Renaissance Italy as the weapon of choice. Today, they more often slay the hearts of men watching a striking Italian woman stride over the cobblestones in her pair by Prada, or are the death of the Italian wannabe who will never manage more than a mincing wobble on a pair of needle-pointed stiletto heels designed by the sadists, Dolce & Gabbana.

Flip-flops are never worn by Italians anywhere except the beach, poolside or at the spa (spa footwear is usually a spa-branded slipper). After leaving the sand

and entering the parking lot or street, shoes or sandals must be worn.

Shower shoes are necessary for any shower that is not your own or is not maintained in the way your mother would disinfect it. Dangerous fungi, molds, and germs lurk, waiting for the Italian foot in public shower stalls and hotel bathtubs.

Upon arrival home, Italians will remove their shoes and put on slippers or some footwear that is designated for the house only. Italians do not wear these slippers down three flights of stairs to retrieve a package from the deliveryman. Italians do not wear slippers to deposit the bundled newspapers and magazines outside the door on recycling day. Bare feet are not allowed in the house. The coolness of the floor can lead to cramps, if not other maladies. Furthermore, between mopping and vacuuming, an errant breeze might bring a dust borne pathogen to settle beneath bare feet and those same feet will slip between clean sheets at bedtime.

***Allora:*** Italian leather shoes are of the finest design and made with the finest craftsmanship. Everyone should own a pair at least once in their life.

# TEENY TINY LOGOS

**Heard in Florence:** "Only an American would wear one of those t-shirts that says *"Ciao Bella.*"

Italians are very subtle in announcing their loyalty through their clothes. Only at the local soccer game do they wear a brash statement of fidelity. No *Università di Firenze* t-shirt or baseball cap with "Venice" emblazoned on it will be part of an Italian's wardrobe.

It was the Italian leather company Bottega Veneta that pioneered the "no logo" luxury purse.

That being said, Italians love logos, but they must be tiny. An Italian woman will be wearing a Versace logo shirt, with Tommy Hilfiger logo slacks, and shoes with the Gucci double G buckle, and a Ferragamo scarf. She will carry a Louis Vuitton bag (real or fake) and wear Armani sunglasses. She will be able to pull all of this off better than a woman of any other nationality.

Better than any other nationality, an Italian man will be able to pull off rich sapphire linen pants by Stefano Ricci, topped with an unstructured Zegna jacket in yellow with a thin blue-green stripe, over a blinding white Brooks Brothers (an Italian brand) shirt and a light-weight Cucinelli cashmere vest (mother always said to keep the tummy warm), a cotton polka-dotted Ferragamo scarf, and Bruno Magli loafers without socks.

***Allora:*** One of the greatest pleasures of visiting Italy is the chance to study italian style outside the pages of a magazine. Take part in the *passeggiata* or sit in the piazza at a café and watch the fashion show that happens every day, everywhere in Italy.

# TERRYCLOTH HOODIES

**Heard at the pool in Trapani:** "*Tesoro*, wrap up and dry your hair. I don't care how hot it is today."

On the beach, at the pool, or after a shower, Italians eschew the bath or beach towel for a thick nubby terrycloth robe with a hood. It may seem surprising that these fashion forward people, who prefer the Speedo or string bikini, all of a sudden nerd-out when drying off. Of course the reason is health-related.

A body glistening with water is a magnet for the blast of air, *colpo d'aria*, which will result in a least a stiff neck, but could escalate to a head cold or pneumonia. Thus, the need for the hood—wet hair cannot be exposed to the fresh air.

The mothers and grandmothers of Italy teach their children at a very young age that it is necessary to become fully dry before exposing any part of the body. Both men and women practice the procedure of wrapping up in the unsexy cocoon before emerging in all of their glory.

***Allora:*** Italian designers such as Frette, Missoni,

305

Armani, and Versace, all create hoody robes. Sears has caught on, offering Americans the "Italian Stallion" cotton robe with hood.

# STYLING THE ITALIAN HEAD

**Heard at the spa in Saturnia:** "Mamma, I want to get my eyebrows waxed. My girlfriend says they are shaggy."

Italian men consume more hair care products, both in terms of variety and amount, than any other culture on earth. Small boys are introduced to hair gel before they are able to walk and will continue the love affair with hair care products late into their 80s—witness Silvio Berlusconi.

Italian women don't fixate on styling products unless the national *alla moda* look-of-the-moment demands it. They will, however, color their hair throughout their entire lives, starting with highlights in their teens. When they hit 60 this often results in a not-found-in-nature red tint also favored by Russian ladies of a certain age.

Italian women have also gotten on the Botox bandwagon and now have little in the way of expressions, happy or sad. The injected fish-lip effect is popular among the wannabe models and television *veline* (scantily clad variety show girls), who hope that Silvio will come to power again and get them a seat in Parliament. The can't-be-too-rich-or-too-thin matrons also love the pillow-lip look.

Men endure the Botox injections for forehead and eyes, but hide the mouth and neck lines under a carefully maintained two-day stubble. They don't seem to realize that when they go gray, the scruff looks more wino than soccer star. The shaved head has not caught on in Italy as an answer to male baldness. The fix of choice seems to be implants or a strange scalp spray-painting procedure (the former Prime Minister Berlusconi did both).

***Allora:*** The "natural" look has never found favor in Italy. Both men and women are sculpted and styled in an idealized look. Sometimes it works, sometimes it amazes, and sometimes it results in cartoonish absurdity.

# ALL DRESSED UP TO GO
# ANYWHERE

**Heard in Assisi:** "Do those Germans think we really want to see their hairy legs and black socks?"

Italians are stylish. This doesn't mean they always pull off the perfect personal look, but they work on it starting at an early age.

There is always time for attention to detail to present the proper appearance to the world. An Italian, woman or man, will not run to the neighborhood pharmacy or newsstand, or even the garbage bin 30 feet from their front door, in sweat pants, a t-shirt and flip-flops. A pair of slacks or skirt, a proper shirt and shoes are necessary for any public appearance—no matter how short a duration or how few people you might encounter. (Remember, there is an extra health-related incentive—flip-flops expose your feet to germs and shoes worn only in the house are never to touch the dirt of the street.)

Italian men and women do not wear shorts in

town, unless the town is at the seaside and it is a month between June and September.

Only foreigners wear large t-shirts with a saying or a picture on it. Italians wear fitted plain t-shirts, perhaps with a small logo. Socks are not worn with sandals, but mini-socks may be worn by men with deck shoes or car shoes or designer athletic shoes to give that sock-free look without the attendant sweaty feet. (They even have a name—*fantasmini*—little ghosts—because you don't see them.)

A popular American blogger once told the story of taking her Italian husband to a restaurant in the U.S. where they were greeted at the front door by a sign that said "No shoes, no shirt, no service." Her Umbrian husband got upset because the eatery was clearly discriminating against the poor. She calmed his shocked sensibilities by explaining that the potential barefooted, bare-chested customers were certainly able to pay, they just lacked an Italian fashion sensibility and a cultural aversion to walking around outside without shoes.

***Allora:*** If an American wishes to "pass" as an Italian for a time, he or she is advised to start the vacation with a quick shopping trip for a couple of head to toe looks designed and made in Italy and then wear nothing else throughout their stay.

# BICYCLING FOR YOUNG AND OLD

**Heard in Florence:** "Was that your 80-year-old mother crossing two lanes of traffic on her bicycle?"

The regional governments all over Italy are pushing for more bicycling, especially in the cities. It is an effort to cut air pollution and traffic congestion in the city streets. Italians are game. They have a history with bikes. The men love the sleek road bikes and the women find that shopping in town goes faster on a bicycle than in a car.

Few women join the men in squeezing into spandex and hitting the hills in the road races that take place every weekend, weather permitting, throughout the central and northern regions of the country. Even men in their 70s and 80s continue riding with their teams.

An old beat up bike is best; less chance of theft. Also, a bicycle with soft wide tires cushions the potholes and ancient stones that make up historic medieval streets.

People of every age ride in the towns: old ladies,

sexy women in stilettos, a guy with the gelled hair balancing his girlfriend sidesaddle in front or behind, lawyers with briefcases, and mothers with their treasured only child in a plastic seat (but no helmet like you would see in the U.S). Every neighborhood has a shop that fixes these aging, rusting bicycles, offering only air for free.

*Allora:* Backroads bicycle tours are the best way to see the countryside of Tuscany and Umbria. Bicycle rental shops fill the needs of those staying for a month or so in cities, large and small.

# SPEED, GLORIOUS SPEED

**Heard on the *autostrada* near Torino:** "What is that tourist doing in the passing lane? Doesn't he see my bright lights flashing?"

Police cars are rarely seen on Italian freeways. Months will go by before you see one on the *autostrada*. Years will go by before you see the police stop a speeding car.

Italians drive fast. They break every posted speed limit. They do not live in fear of the police car parked behind the big sign announcing the next Autogrill, or in the blind spot over the hill, or in the median between the lanes of traffic. It never happens.

Highway cops are at their leisure in Italy. They like to congregate on a scenic country road and wave cars over with their lollypop signs (a white stick with a round red top, perfectly sized for sticking in the boot of a motorcycle *polizia*) to check if the insurance is paid up or the passengers are wearing seat belts, or there are snow chains and a florescent vest in the trunk, even if it is August.

Cameras in small metal boxes on the roadside monitor excessive speed. There will be a warning sign a few meters before the camera, but most likely some speedster living in the area has already painted over the lens, so Italians don't worry too much about a fine for speeding. Fate will play a big part in whether a ticket will come in the mail in a month or so.

The superhero spatial sense that all Italians under the age of 80 seem to have while driving is uncanny. The skill of driving fast in tight and winding medieval alleys in the center of ancient towns or on the serpentine roads in the Tuscan hills or the one-lane-used-as-two-lane *strade* that cling to the cliffs of Cinque Terre or Amalfi, is hardwired into their DNA. Forward or in reverse they never lose a mirror or scrape a bumper or demolish an oncoming car. No other nationality seems to have this heightened power.

On the other hand, Italians, the descendants of Galileo and Fermi, do not seem to have an understanding of physics. Maybe they don't study it in middle school and after that the testosterone kicks in, wiping the lesson out of the little gray cells. As a refresher: the ability of a car to safely stop starts with the perception and the reaction time. The distance covered during this time increases with speed: distance = rate x time. Good so far?

Now, given that Italians have a heightened perception and reaction time, the only problem is speed, right? Wrong. If the distance is small and the speed is great, disaster ensues.

Italians tailgate. It seems to have little t testosterone because Italian women tailgate, ⸺ little to do if they have anywhere to be. Italians out for a Sunday jaunt, having nothing special to do and nowhere they have to be, drive very very fast right on the bumper of the car in front of them. It has little to do with the type of road they are on. The only difference is, can you get out of their way?

An indignant Italian will claim that tourists must realize that it is imperative to tailgate on a two-lane road because one never knows when there will be a short space to pass. On a freeway the foreigners are just stupid if they don't keep to the right-hand lane—as if tailgating only goes on in the passing lane. An Italian will get a "figure the odds" look when someone proposes hypotheticals of a blown tire, a sheep on the road, a pothole, or a Californian tourist stepping into a crosswalk.

Italians like to average 100 kilometers per hour (about 60 miles per hour) except on the freeway, when only 150 kilometers per hour will do. They will drive at this speed at a distance of three meters (nine feet) from the back bumper of the car in front of them. At 100 kilometers per hour, it takes the average Fiat, Ford, Alfa Romeo, or BMW between 37 meters and 40 meters (about 121 to 130 feet) to stop.

***Allora:*** As a foreigner, you must learn the physics lesson for the Italians and get out of their way. Do not raise your middle finger to comment—road rage will ensue.

# No Guts, No Crossing

**Heard at a cross-walk in Rome:** "Wait until some Italians come and then do what they do. We're going to get killed on our own."

Foreigners seem to think a crosswalk denotes pedestrian right-of-way in Italy, especially if the little green man on the traffic light is shining bright. Do not be lulled into such faulty reasoning. The only place pedestrians have the right-of-way in Italy is in Venice.

Even in the *area pedonale* (the pedestrian malls) of Siena, Florence, Assisi and Perugia, taxis, tourist vans, city buses, bicycles, police cars, emergency vehicles, and illegal drivers of both scooters and cars, share the space and have priority because of their size and speed. A tourist will never win the battle.

Approaching a crosswalk with people present with the intent to cross, an Italian driver is most likely to speed up so as to not inconvenience the pedestrians unnecessarily. Or he will swerve around the group to allow equal access. But stop? Never. Unless there is a red light against him *and* there is the possibility of traffic coming from another direction *or* in the unlikely event that a police officer is present *and* looking in the right direction, then the driver may *think* about stopping.

**Allora:** The pedestrian is never right and never has the right-of-way in Italy. Get used to it!

# THE RULES OF THE ITALIAN LINE

**Heard at the bank:** "Hey, I was here first. Didn't you see me here before I stepped out for a smoke?"

Italian lines (or queues, as the British say) can be found all over the world, everywhere four or more Italians are waiting for something. Outside of Italy, they are most often observed in airports, but they can occur anywhere. Like Italian design, Italian lines do not have a clear beginning or an end; they are a work of art.

An Italian line never looks like a line. It is more of a competition. The goal is to get to the front first. The best players are little old ladies with canes. The next best is a little old lady without a cane. They win because they never waste time pretending that they are not trying to cut the line.

A single player has more finesse than a group. An individual Italian will wander seemingly without purpose along the outside of the line, occasionally appearing to pair up with one or more people in the line, and then move forward again, bettering his position all the while.

319

A group of Italians will rush the line, pushing those in front to the side and forward until the non-Italians step out of the way. This is deadly serious, especially when shopping carts are involved at the door of a supermarket. If only Italians are involved, not one of them will give way.

Perhaps it is just a definitional problem: The Italian word for line is *coda*. *Coda* in Italian also refers to the tail of an animal and therefore, by definition, is something that moves back and forth; not something static or straight or "in line" as the Americans would understand it.

At a bank or a post office, if only Italians are present, there will be no line, just a jockeying for position with attendant comments on the process: "Why is there only one window open? I'll ask for help at the desk." Or excuses will be used to achieve a better position: "I just have a quick question." (What is left unsaid is that in her purse are ten Christmas cards to four different continents that need postage.)

Italians, however, have patience for the Italian line. It's a karmic thing: "Today I don't need to get into the movie theater immediately, so I will let two people cut in front of me in line. Next month, I may have to get through security faster at the airport, and I will be given some slack." Or "someday I will be old, so I will let the old man with the old dog order his coffee before me at the bar."

Italians see Americans and Japanese as easy marks in the line competition. Americans have an exaggerated sense of personal space and will move before coming in contact with a stranger and are also known to be easy-going. The Japanese lose because even though they are competitive in line, they won't be confrontational.

The two nationalities that give Italians the most trouble are the British, who carry the traditional orderly queue philosophy away from World War II and won't let go of it, and the Germans, who love being right, keep track of their place in the world, love confrontation, and will defend that place to the end.

The large city post offices have decided to solve the queuing problem by offering machines that spit out numbers on a piece of paper. Easy, you think? Ticket A101 goes before ticket A102. But what about B101? The list beside each button on the machines describe the many and various services offered by the post offices: Italians pay their bills at the post office (the postal service is not trusted to convey an envelope with a check inside to the gas company), obtain their pension checks (the elderly do not trust direct deposit), apply for visas (the application *only,* visas are not *issued* at the post office), buy stamps, register verified mailings, send packages, etc.

It is the post office ticketing machine that offers the perfect opportunity for the Italian to practice his queue-jumping skills. An Italian will take two tickets— one for the A windows and one for the B windows— because he knows that the postal workers at each and every window can do the A tasks and the B tasks. All he needs to say is "I was confused about which ticket I should take ..."

Visitors to Italy should certainly observe and defend their positions in the Italian line. They may even want to attempt the maneuvers of the Italian practitioners, but tourists should be aware that they are competing with pros, who have practiced the moves since they could toddle.

***Allora:*** One of the greatest joys of the long-term visitor to Italy is to beat a bunch of Italians in a game of Italian Line.

# BUTCHER SHOP CHAIRS

**Heard in Montalcino:** "Have a seat. I'll be with you after I serve these two ladies."

Why are there chairs in the butcher shop? To rest the weary shopper while waiting for a personal consultation with the man himself. It may take you 30 minutes or more to be served in the butcher shop or the cheese shop or the pasta shop or at the post office or the doctor's office. The chairs are a hint. Ask around to find out who was the last to enter and then sit down. Once that "last" person is served it will be your turn.

When you are given an audience with the butcher or cheese monger, you will get 100 percent of his attention . . . for as long as you want. Thus, the need for chairs.

This is most apparent in food shops, but can happen in a bank, a hardware store, a post office, or a visa office. You may conduct whatever business you have, buy whatever you need, and also have a conversation comprising of five or six topics.

It doesn't help to be impatient. Sit down and listen. You'll catch up on the gossip. In the 15 to 30 minutes that you wait patiently, you will have learned all of the latest news in the village, either given to you directly by others sitting in the adjoining chairs or by eavesdropping on the butcher's conversation with his other customers.

Once it is your turn, you can discuss the weather, your own health, the butcher's health, the health of your respective family members, the cuts of meat you might want to consider, the recipes that go with each cut, the wine pairing that is appropriate, the shape of your vineyards, the potential outcome of the soccer team's game that night, the sorry history of the team over the last few weeks, the affair one of the previous customers is having with the banker, and any other subject that has not been covered after you entered the shop.

None of the occupants of the three chairs will try to interfere with your "moment". They are all listening in as intently as you were 30 minutes before.

***Allora:*** For the multi-tasking visitor to Italy, the experience will slow even the most type-A+ person down. There is no way to rush. If you get one task done a day that is normal. Complete two tasks, you are an overachiever. Three tasks, you are either cheating or you are a hero.

# TO TIP OR NOT TO TIP

**Heard in Milan:** American, looking at the credit card slip for dinner, "Where do I put the tip?"

Italians pay *coperto*. Italians don't tip. Given the size of most Italian homes and the closed private world of *la famiglia*, it is no wonder that Italians socialize in public. Foreigners should not take offense if they are not invited into an Italian friend's home for a meal. It's nothing personal.

The effect of socializing in public is that meals in a restaurant, trattoria or pizzeria are likely to be long, drawn-out affairs. The group at the table is not only purchasing food from the kitchen, they are purchasing time at the table—renting space for a social activity. In an Italian restaurant, therefore, the concept of "turning tables" does not exist. Actually the hardest item to get brought to the table in a timely manner is the bill.

Don't confuse *coperto* with *servizio*. *Servizio* is the word for "tip." You will rarely find *servizio* as a line item on your dinner check and you won't find a space for it on the credit card slip. Italians don't tip. This probably stems from a time when all restaurants were family operations, where the family shared in the profits. The bill for *coperto*, food and beverages was inclusive of service.

*Coperto* is the "rent" that is paid for the table. It means "cover" and is arguably the cost of the table-cloth and napkins (or the cleaning thereof), the place-mats, the bread and the condiments, but in reality it is the cost of keeping the table as long as is wanted. (If you don't think you pay for these "cover" items in the rest of the world, just ask a restaurateur where they recoup their overhead costs.)

Another reason that there is no culture of tipping is that waiters are paid a living wage in Italy. Waiters are professionals, who view their jobs as lifelong vocations, not something they are doing until they finish school, get a career-making part in a theater play, or write the next blockbuster. In Italy, waiters aren't paid just a minimum wage, living on hope that the tips will cover the rent bill and the gas money.

As professionals not dependent on customer largesse, waiters are not paid to be a friend. Unless the customer is a "regular" of many years standing, the waiter will be efficient, but distant. He is there to serve food and wine, not chat with the customers. "Hi, I'm your waiter Gregorio. How can I help you?" "How were those *spaghetti alle vongole*?" "Is everything all right, here?" "Is there anything else I can get for you?" These are phrases that will never be uttered by an Italian waiter. He will bring the food and get out of the way so that the customers can do what they came to do—

socialize with family and friends.

If the evening has been fabulous an Italian may leave some change on the table. It is a token message of satisfaction.

***Allora:*** The visitor to Italy should not become stressed over the issue of tipping. Use some knowledge of the Italian custom to guide your decisions.

# Do You Have Change

**Heard in any *gelateria*:** "Are you sure you don't have a one euro coin?"

*"Mi dispiace, non ho spiccioli."* ("I'm sorry I don't have any coins.") has become one of my favorite phrases in Italian. After 15 years, I say it just to spite Italian cashiers, even if I have plenty of coins. In Italy, you never know when you are really going to need small bills and coins, so you hoard them. It's part of becoming Italian.

"What's the deal with change in Italy?" asks the tourist after a mere two days in the country. At the *gelateria*, the newsstand, the post office, museum, and not last nor least, the coffee bar, the customer is quizzed about the possibility of *spiccioli* (coins), so that no *resto* (change) is necessary. The person at the cash register is willing to wait until you go through all of your pockets and the bottom of your purse in search of 20 *centesimi* (cents) or a one euro coin.

Coinage seems to be a rare commodity in almost any shop, eatery, or even the government-run entities in Italy. You may be denied the opportunity to buy a newspaper or candy bar if you pull out a 50 euro bill. Even a five euro bill will garner frowns if you are purchasing an 80 *centesimi* espresso.

Italian vending machines don't give change, despite the fact that there is a coin return slot. Be prepared to round up if you really need that Coke or bottle of water.

The problem seems to stem from the Italians' dislike of dealing with their banks. Understandable. No one, absolutely no one, wants to deal with the bureaucratic hassles and time suck of the Italian bank, least of all the small business person. A visit to the bank only invites the headache of poor service and a paper trail, two things sought to be avoided by all Italians. But this still doesn't answer why there is such a hassle regarding change when you are buying stamps or tickets from money mills like the post office or the Uffizi Gallery?

In the 1970s, Italy literally ran out of coins. Banks issued what were called *mini-assegni*" or "mini-checks" that took the place of change. These mini-checks looked like *Monopoly* money to replace the small denomination coins that were in short supply. It was not until 1978 that the Italian government produced coins in large enough quantities to meet consumer demand.

Even the priest of two tiny churches in the center of Florence goes to the Jewish-owned grocery store in the neighborhood with his sacks of donation coins to get the amount converted into large denomination

bills. It's a win-win—there is no pape
priest and the store gets a replenished s
coins. And neither has to enter the enca
rity door of the local bank.

*Allora:* Don't ask why, just carry change.

# BEWARE OF BANKS

**Heard in any Italian bank:** "No we don't change dollars here."

Italy has the oldest bank in the world. It was established in Siena in 1472. It's called Monte de' Paschi di Siena. Never mind that due to some catastrophic, and perhaps criminal, decisions made in 2010, the bank needed a five billion euro bailout. Not to worry, the Italian government will never let MPS fail. The nation's pride rests on having the oldest bank.

The Medici of Florence created the first banking system—an international chain of banks that stretched all over Europe.

With all of this history, one would think that the Italians would perfect the banking experience. Instead it seems that Italian banks are a microcosm of all of Italy's fears and foibles.

Start with the door. Banks are not welcoming. They don't invite you in to deposit your money. Instead, to get into the Italian bank you must enter a capsule—one person at a time. You push the button to get

333

the cylinder's door open. You step inside. You push the button to close the door and trap yourself inside and you hope and pray that the inner door opens—just a moment or two of claustrophobic panic. Some of the cylinders require you to leave a fingerprint scan before it will allow you in. Is it to discourage bank robbers or customers?

Once inside, don't look for the line. Italians don't queue. There will be presumptive customers milling about. They will know when it's their turn. One may step out for a smoke and then come back expecting that his place in the disorder has been maintained. But then the little old lady with a cane, the man "with just one quick question", the mother with the fretting baby, and the business man with the expensive watch, will all cut in front of the unwary. Someone will go stand between the teller windows to slide into place "just for a moment."

The milling crowd may contain a person who has a favorite teller—"the one from Sicily is nice, the Florentine is a bitch" or "I want to deal with the man." If the teller is really a favorite, the conversation will start with pleasantries, go on to the weather, meld into a bit of banking business, and end with a description of last night's dinner, all while the milling crowd grows.

Banking involves paperwork. Do not imagine that automation has cut down on the paper in Italian banks. Yes, there will be two-finger typing, but then there will be printing, stamping with an official rubber stamp, copying in triplicate, signatures and initials. You will

need your bank card, your identity card
*fiscale*. If you are a foreigner, you will a...
port and your *permesso di soggiorno*. Without the ...
will not be able to open a bank account. But do you
really want the joy of an Italian bank account?

**Allora:**   Do not come to Italy with traveler's
checks. Do not plan to change dollars into euro. Come
with at least 50 euro in cash. Come with two diverse
credit cards. Come with an ATM card (known in Italy
as a Bancomat card) for which you know the PIN code.
If you can make it through your vacation without entering an Italian bank, you will be a happier person.

# NO SERVICE WITH A SMILE

**Heard in Venice:** "No we do not accept returned merchandise."

"The customer is always right" is not an Italian slogan, but *caveat emptor* is. There is rarely any desire expressed in Italy to engage in customer service. Also, there is no Italian word for browsing. In most shops the selection is neither deep nor broad. Returns are not accepted. In short, shopping in Italy is not fun—it is a challenge.

The shop assistant, *la commessa,* is not your friend. He or she is not available to make your shopping experience fun. They are there to greet you—*buongiorno* or *buonasera*—and they expect an equal response or they write you off as rude. Then, their job to leave you alone unless you have a specific question or request. If the *commessa* offers more, she is not Italian.

An Italian shop assistant is not going to follow you around and ask "May I help you?" They have telephone calls to make, cigarettes to smoke and manicures to finish. Their official responsibilities are: to know what the inventory contains (because it will not be displayed); to have an in-depth knowledge of the items for sale (information rarely shared); and to take your money and bag the item. They will usually be good at two out of the three.

These are the activities a *commessa* does not think is part of her job description: to fold anything you unfold (witness the frown as you unwrap sweater after sweater); to accept returns (against store policy, even if bought the same day); to follow you around; to tell you something you try on looks good when it doesn't; to gift wrap a present; or to have sufficient change.

The sign on the door *"entrata libera"* is confusing to most foreigners and it is impossible to get a clear explanation of the phrase from an Italian. A direct translation is "enter free." Perhaps it goes back to that problem of having no Italian word for browsing. *"Entrata libera"* is as close to offering to allow you to enter and look around without a guarantee that you will buy anything. It is not an offer of service. It is simply an expression that the door is open and you may go in.

Like waiters in Italy, shopkeepers are meant to be professionals in their field. They are not students or want-to-be actors or failed novelists or someone rising into the ranks of management or ownership. They probably have an employment contract for life. They cannot be fired and they are not working on commission. They have no motivation to assist you to improve your shopping experience.

You will not find a bargain basement style of store

in Italy—one of those where masses of discounted merchandise is thrown into a bin for customers to paw through. Italians find this undignified and slightly unsanitary. This leads directly to the shop assistant attitude that the customer is not to fondle the goods, dig through the precisely arranged racks, or unfold each size of cashmere sweater looking for one that just might fit an American frame. The disarray that follows the tourist around the store is upsetting to the *commessa* and she will let you know it.

Your job as a customer is to have decided what you want before you enter the store, perhaps by studying the contents in the window. You greet the *commessa* politely. You should know the color and the size of the item and express the wish clearly so that the *commessa* can either find it for you in the shop or in storage behind the counter. You will have exact change or, in the alternative, have informed your credit card company that you will be shopping in Italy (do not expect assistance if your card is refused). You say "*Grazie*" upon receipt of the store's bag (do not ask to place the item in a bag with another store's logo). You will accept all risk for mistakes in judgment, size, number of items, color, and quality.

*Allora:* Happy shopping. Not.

# SALUTING THE FLAG

**Heard in Milan:** "We have nothing in common with anyone living south of Florence."

In the U.S., Americans display their flag at every opportunity. In France, there is a fierce effort to retain the purity of the French language. In Japan, the national identity excludes all other races and cultures. The only time the Italians become patriotic is when their national soccer team, the *Azzurri*, is playing in the World Cup. In fact, at any time, there are more blue soccer team flags flying in Italy than the green, red and white national flag.

Why isn't the soccer team decked out in the national colors? Three reasons: the team had its start in 1910 when Italy was ruled by the Savoy kings and the monarch's color was blue; Mussolini changed the color of the national soccer team uniforms to fascist black; and after the king was banished and the dictator was hung out to dry, people wanted to remember a better time and returned to Azzurri blue.

Italians are leery of patriotism. This also goes

back to the fascist period. Mussolini demanded a simplistic fanatical nationalistic loyalty and we all know how that worked out. After World War II, Italians rejected that philosophy and returned to a more city-centric, family-oriented form of allegiance.

Visitors should also remember that Italy is a very young republic. Its history is in the city-states created, fought over, and, for many, constantly in a state of flux for over seven centuries. Unification of the country occurred just over 150 years ago in 1861.

Today, an Italian is more likely to claim to be Florentine first; Tuscan second; from central Italy third; before placing himself in the national pool—until the World Cup rolls around, again.

***Allora:*** Italians have an ambivalent attitude toward American patriotism. On one hand, they see it as naive. In the alternative, they are envious of stability of the U.S. government and way the country pulls together in times of difficulty.

# THE WELCOME MAT IS NOT OUT

**Heard in Torino:** "Those in Milan once called the Florentines 'those Africans', and the Florentines said the same about the Romans, the Romans said something similar about the Neapolitans, but the Neapolitans ascribed it to the Sicilians. Here it ended because the people to the south of Sicily were actually Africans."

It was the gaffe heard around the globe. Just two days after Barack Obama's historic election victory, the world's collective jaw dropped when Silvio Berlusconi quipped that the next U.S. President was "young, handsome and even has a good tan." Though the Italian Prime Minister refused to apologize for the failed attempt at humor, Obama and his aides gave Berlusconi a pass. It is Berlusconi who would not let the incident rest. He called his critics "imbeciles," saying the remark was meant as a compliment.

The conventional wisdom in Italy, in both press and political circles, seemed to be that it's just Berlusconi being Berlusconi. But that's telling in itself. In many ways, mainstream Italian society is several generations behind the rest of the West when it comes to race. In supposedly polite company, one can still hear a cleaning woman often generically referred to as a *"Filippina"* and Northern Italians joke that darker-skinned southerners are "Moroccans."

Cecile Kyenge is a strong woman. She had to be. As Italy's first black cabinet minister, she had to endure a string of repeated racist, sexist and sexually violent insults. Kyenge, an eye doctor and Italian citizen married to an Italian, was born in the Democratic Republic of Congo; she moved to Italy when she was a teen to continue her studies. After being elected to office, she was named Minister of Integration by Prime Minister Enrico Letta in 2012. Kyenge, who can relate to the experience of those moving to Italy for opportunity, favored legislation that would allow children born in Italy to immigrant parents to get automatic citizenship. That was a change in a country where nationality is judged more on blood than birth.

Soon after her appointment, the insults started. Roberto Calderoli, a member of Italy's Senate from the anti-immigration Northern League party, said at a political rally: "I love animals—bears and wolves, as everyone knows—but when I see the pictures of Kyenge I cannot but think of, even if I'm not saying she is one, the features of an orangutan."

Kyenge, responded that she is proud to be black and Italian and that the threats were "not worthy of our Italy." When someone threw bananas at her during a speech, she called it sad and a waste of food.

One of Italy's old self-images was "*Italiani brava gente*" – Italians are decent folk. But that ingrained idea is being challenged by recent events and history. Recently, Roma soccer fans shouted racist insults at Milan's Mario Balotelli, who is black, and also one of Italy's national squad's top strikers.

In 1938, Italy passed the Racial Laws that discriminated against Italian Jews. After the Second World War, Italians looked at racially motivated violence in the U.S. and Britain, complimenting themselves on not being racist "like the Anglo-Saxons." While there were no race riots or lynching in Italy, there were also few nonwhites until the last two decades.

Until the new millennium, Italy was best known as a source of migrants to other countries. An estimated 24 million Italians emigrated abroad between 1876 and 1976.

Since 2000, many immigrants have integrated, set up businesses, become citizens and come to expect equal treatment. In 2011, there were more than 4.5 million foreign nationals registered as resident in Italy— mainly Asians, Africans and Eastern Europeans—as against 1.5 million only eight years earlier.

After the 2008 world economic crisis, the Italian economy entered years of recession and the number of jobs decreased for all, especially the young. The brain-drain of emigrating young, educated Italians became a new national concern.

Most Italians would be horrified to be called racist,

but they are slow to accept the new reality that a "melt-ing pot" society will bring the country renewed eco-nomic strength. There is still a long way to go before a black cabinet minister or black soccer player is consid-ered truly "Italian."

**Allora:** Unfortunately, the group of Americans most blatantly affected by the racism of some ill-bred Italians is that of the female African American college student trying to enjoy her semester abroad. She will find herself subjected to unwanted attention and com-ments by Italian men who view her as a prostitute. This is the result of ongoing human trafficking of African women into Europe for work in the sex-trades.

# WHO IS IN CHARGE

**Heard in Rome:** "What happened during the no-confidence vote this morning?"

Sixty-three governments in 68 years, with 27 different Prime Ministers—so why in 2014 should Italy care that it has a new government, with yet another Prime Minister, Matteo Renzi? It can seem like a merry-go-round: the people on the painted horses change, but sometimes not, and when the music stops Italy is in the same place. In the past 20 years, Italy's problems have remained depressingly familiar: a stagnating economy, an enormous national debt, high unemployment, a large, inefficient bureaucracy, and a political and educational system that discourages initiative, innovation, merit, and opportunity.

Some say Italy is a country that has devolved into a gerontocracy: positions of power are occupied by men in their 60s, and 70s. Just recently with the advent of Prime Minister Renzi and Beppe Grillo's Five Star Movement, younger faces have appeared in Parliament. According to the Italian Constitution, the citizens do not vote directly for the Prime Minister. They vote for the Parliament, choosing a party that if victorious will seat representatives in the two houses of Parliament, the Senate and the House. Then the Parliament, through the powers of the President, nominates the Prime Minister, who selects the members of the Government (Ministers of Finance, State, Culture, etc.).

Currently, there are 945 members of Parliament (630 in the House and 315 in the Senate)—more than twice the number in the U.S., for a country with one-fifth the population. There are also at any one time, depending on the whim of the President and death, up to five senators-for-life. Usually, this job with its $250,000 salary goes to people in their 70s, the latest being architect Renzo Piano, age 76 at the time of his appointment in 2013. But scientist Elena Cattaneo was 51 at the time of her appointment, filling the seat left by Rita Levi-Montalcini, who died at the age of 103 while still serving as a senator.

Prime Minister Renzi was not voted into office. He became Prime Minister of a Government, called "*delle larghe intese*", that contained members of different parties (left, right and center) and was established in a situation of emergency, without any specific election, in order to save the country from a political default. He is the second Prime Minister since 2011 to be given the position without electoral input.

While the old men of the Parliament enjoy their big salaries and exploit their expense accounts, Italian youth unemployment is above 40 percent. The job market is bifurcated between extraordinarily well-protected older workers who cannot be fired and younger people working on "precarious" temporary contracts, often making about 1,000 euros (less than $1,400) a month. A huge percentage of young people live at home well into their 30s, waiting for a full-time job.

The most ambitious and energetic seek their fortunes overseas—in the U.K., France, or the U.S. Young Italian academics are finding professorial and research positions in American universities, discovering that it is easier to break into the U.S. system than that of their own country, which functions, much like the country's political system, according to the principles of cronyism, nepotism and seniority.

***Allora:*** Italians used to joke that they were a colony of the United States, given the large numbers of Italian who emigrated after the two world wars. Those Italians left because they could not afford to feed their families. Today, food is plentiful, but jobs are not, but the effect is the same.

# STRIKES FOR EVERY OCCASION

**Heard in Rome on a stationary bus packed with passengers:** "Is this one of the emergency buses running during *lo sciopero*? Where is the driver?"

As the tourist season starts in Italy, the savvy visitor knows to keep in mind that one of the Italian national pastimes is to go on strike. Some years see more of *lo sciopero* than others, but in difficult economic and political times in Italy it is certain to be a country filled with delays and inconvenience.

*Lo Sciopero* is a strike or temporary work stoppage. A *sciopero* can be national, regional, or local and can affect only one service sector or many. They inconvenience everyone and help no one, but Italians keep exercising their right to strike.

The most common strikes are local, usually lasting from four hours to one day. Strikes often involve the transportation sector. They are almost invariably announced in advance, which at least helps alert travelers to plan around the dates of strikes and arrange alternative modes of transportation. Occasionally, to make things more complicated, they are cancelled or post-poned at short notice.

There are many rail strikes in Italy. They generally take place at the weekend, from Saturday evening until Sunday evening. The law guarantees a minimum service, so some trains should still run. There are also frequent strikes of urban transport. These *scioperi* are generally announced in advance, and many city transport authorities will try to negotiate continuation of service during the rush hour to help commuters.

A large proportion of Italy's air travel strikes have involved Alitalia, the perpetually troubled Italian national airline. Sometimes there are more wide-ranging strikes by ground staff or by air traffic controllers, and unfortunately there's not much travelers can do about this, other than be patient. These strikes usually last several hours; sometimes they simply delay flights, at other times they can lead to cancellations.

Other strikes in Italy – by schoolteachers, students, taxi drivers, garbage collectors, tobacco sellers, even bloggers (in 2009 to protest a restrictive bill in Parliament) add to the ever-growing variety of *Scioperi Italiani*. Strikes may even occur in sympathy with strikers from other countries.

Work stoppages by state employees may affect museum openings. Strikes at individual museums will almost always be timed to back-up against the weekly closed day. Strikes in any industry happen almost every year in the week leading up to and after the national

August 15th holiday. Helpfully, the *Commissione di Garanzia Sciopero* tracks all of the national, regional, and local strikes and lists them on detailed online spreadsheets.

The granddaddy of all strikes is the national strike (*lo sciopero nazionale*), also known as a general strike, when all transportation may be stopped or experience a slow-down. Garbage won't be collected, museums will be closed, and many stores, including supermarkets will be closed. National strikes are fairly rare, but it's a day on which most Italians know it is hopeless to try to get anything done. It's better to stay home and catch up on sleep, read a good book or try out that new recipe for slow-cooking *peposo di cinghiale*.

**Allora:** A tourist in Italy has little chance to know before a strike occurs to avoid the consequent inconvenience, but a general awareness that they won't last long may help.

# THE EVIL EYE AND THE DEVIL'S HORN

**Heard in Rome:** "Get that hat off the bed. You want to bring death to visit?"

The first use of the Latin *superstitio* is found in the writing of the historians Livy and Ovid (1st century BC). At that time the term "superstition" was used in Italy mostly in the negative sense of an excessive fear of the gods or unreasonable religious belief, as opposed to *religio*, the proper, reasonable awe of the gods. The term *superstitio*, or *superstitio vana* (vain superstition), was applied by Tacitus and Domitian (80 AD) to those religious cults (Druids, early Christianity) in the Roman Empire that were officially outlawed.

Throughout history, Italian culture has been rich with superstitions for good or evil that continue to form the basis of many of the Italian Life Rules. Today a visitor may be surprised at which superstitions are taken seriously and which are taken with a grain of salt, so to speak.

### The Evil Eye (*Malocchio*)

The Evil Eye is one of the most ancient superstitions in Italy. Every region seems to have their own version of the Evil Eye, but some take it more seriously than others. One thing they seem to have in common is that the Evil Eye is caused by jealousy and envy.

### The Devil's Horn (*Corno*)

The use of the *Corno*, or Devil's Horn, is a curse of impotency or of the cuckold. The twisted phallic red coral, gold or silver amulet (*cornicello*) is often worn or carried by men to ward off curses on their "manliness" or "mojo". Although many claim the amulet represents one of the horns of the devil, the *Corno* predates Christianity by thousands of years.

Related to the *Corno* is the hand gesture (extending only the pinkie and index finger like a pair of horns) known as the *mano cornuta*, which can be used (pointing upwards or directly at the victim (*cornuto*)) to curse another or not so subtly send the message that a man's wife or girlfriend is straying, and can also be used to ward off the Evil Eye (pointing fingers down).

### Lucky Numbers

The number 13 is lucky in Italy, especially when gambling. The number 13 is also associated with the Goddess of Fertility and the lunar cycles, and is thought to bring prosperity and abundant life. Although the number 13 is considered lucky, sitting down to a table with 12 others is an ill omen. At the Last Supper, Jesus ate with his 12 disciples before one of them, Judas Iscariot, betrayed him. Italians aim to avoid a similar turning of the tables.

### Unlucky Numbers

The number 17 is considered unlucky. Italians dislike the number so much that some hotels don't have a 17th level. The phobia has to do with how it is written. When the number 17 is written using Roman numerals XVII, it can be rearranged to spell the Roman word VIXI meaning "I have lived" and is found on ancient tombstones, thus tempting death. When written using Arabic numerals, the number 17 is still considered unlucky since it resembles a man (the 1) hanging from a gallows (the 7).

### Superstitions Pertaining to Bread

A loaf of bread must always be placed face up, or else bad luck will come. Again, some claim this has a basis in Christianity with the symbol of Christ as the Bread of Life. It is impolite to turn the bread upside-down or to stab a knife into a loaf of bread. Bread is considered a staple of life and so every precaution was taken in order to prevent cursing the supply.

### Blessing or Exorcising a New House

The blessing or exorcism of a new house in Italy is still practiced, especially when it comes to newly-weds. Moving into a first home was accompanied by the necessary rituals to rid the place of any spirits that may have been left by the previous owners and could harm the new couple or their first child. A new broom is a common first gift to sweep away evil spirits. Salt sprinkled in the corners of the house will purify it. Neighborhood priests go house to house before Easter to bless each home with holy water (in modern times a tiny note is frequently wedged in the door to notify the residents of the service).

### Marriage Superstitions

Singles, don't let a broom touch your feet when someone is cleaning the floors. If you do, you will never be swept off your feet and get married. Likewise, never sweep over the feet of an unmarried person, or they will never marry.

### Cats – Good and Bad

It's bad luck to have a black cat cross your path. On the other hand, it's considered good fortune if you happen to hear a cat sneeze.

### What Not to Put on a Bed

Don't put a hat on a bed. Traditionally, when the sick were on their deathbeds a priest would come to receive their final confessions. The priest would remove his hat and set it on the bed so that he could put on the vestments. Thus, a hat's temporary resting place is associated with eternal rest, a thought that keeps Italians from sleeping peacefully.

A bed should never face the door because it replicates the position of a coffin in a church. Other unlucky items to keep off the bed are hangers, hairbrushes, and shoes (of course the last is a hygiene issue, too).

## A Toast Full of Bad Luck

Never raise a toast with a glass full of water as it is bad luck. Don't cross arms when you clink wine glasses together. Also, be sure to look fellow toasters in the eye when clinking glasses and don't slip up by forgetting to take a sip before setting your drink down otherwise you will have seven years of bad sex.

## Spills of All Kinds

Don't spill salt or olive oil for fear of bad luck. This conception may have begun as a trick to motivate people to handle the previously expensive goods with care. If it happens, however, toss a bit of salt over each shoulder or rub a drop of olive oil behind each ear. If you spill wine at the dinner table, wet your fingers and dab some behind every person's ear.

## Hearses – Coming and Going

Don't follow a hearse that isn't carrying a coffin. You are in death's wake and soon people might be attending your funeral. However, if the hearse bears a body, it isn't in pursuit of another passenger, so you are safe, just like if you pass a hearse driving in the opposite direction.

## A Word to the Wise

Never trim toe and fingernails on a Thursday.

Don't start a journey, new project or get married on a Friday or a Tuesday.

Never give chrysanthemums as a gift; they are only for the graveyard.

Have your hair cut during the new moon.

Never get a perm during your menstrual cycle.

Eat lentils on New Year's Day and money will follow during the year.

If you give a gift of a new wallet, always put at least a coin in it.

To prevent a downturn of fortune, people practice *tocca ferro* and touch iron if they think something bad is going to occur. Italian men, knowing what must be protected at all costs, may tap their testicles, known as *tocca palle*. This is similar to knocking on wood.

<u>Good Omens</u>

Seeing a spider at night is a sure sign of monetary income.

When you drop something, someone is thinking of you and their name starts with the first letter of item dropped. (Drop a pen (*penna*) and Pamela is thinking of you.)

When your nose itches, it's either "*pugni o baci*": punches or kisses.

Finding a button on the ground: a new friendship is on the horizon.

Dream of someone dying and you will have added ten years to their life.

When a new moon appears, the minute you see it say the New Moon Incantation: "*Benvenuta Luna che mi porti fortuna!*" – "Welcome, moon and may you bring me good fortune!" This is to be repeated bowing respectfully at the lunar sliver 13 times with a coin in each hand.

<u>Bad Omens</u>

Killing a spider will take money away.

Breaking a mirror will result in seven years of bad luck.

Giving a handkerchief as a gift will bring tears.

Crossing silverware on the table foretells strife.

Passing each other the salt hand to hand (without putting it down on the table) will lead to an imminent fight between the two.

Walking under a ladder.

Crossing arms when shaking hands in a group.

An owl sighting is a vision of the spirits of the dead.

***Allora:*** The edicts of pagan Roman gods and goddesses still vie with the teachings of Catholic saints to create a rich broth of superstitions to scare and cheer Italians in their daily lives.

# LEARNING LANGUAGE

**Heard in the expat community in Florence:** "Why can't Italians speak English?"

This is Italy and the national language is Italian. English-speaking visitors must get over the idea that a popular tourist destination must provide services in English. Most Italian citizens will never need to speak another language. Except in time of extreme economic crisis (world war, international banking collapse), Italians don't tend to leave their home region.

English grammar is different from Italian grammar, therefore many terms are difficult to translate into English. Other languages, such as Danish, Swedish, and Norwegian, have a similar grammar to English, thus there is a great deal of congruency.

Something that was absolutely beautiful in Italian may become heinously awkward in English, or very difficult to understand, or untranslatable. Try putting a paragraph of Italian written with proper grammar into

Google Translate and see what comes out on the other side. That is what is going on in the head of an Italian starting to learn English.

There is a greater difference in meaning (and therefore a greater loss of meaning in translation) between English and the romance languages. For Scandinavians, learning English is more a matter of memorizing equivalent words, while for romance language native speakers learning English is also a matter of learning new ways to express themselves. For instance, in Swedish "*kyss mig*" is "kiss me" in English, "*kan du höra mig?*" is the same as "can you hear me?" and "*det är kallt*" is the Swedish for "it is cold."

If it were just about education, then some Italians would speak English well and others not. It is rare to find an Italian who speaks perfect grammatically correct English, even among those holding prestigious international positions, unless they spent their university years in England or the U.S., have lived for an extended period of time in an English-speaking country, have a spouse or partner who is an original English-speaker, or learned the language as a child and continues to use it on a regular basis.

For the visitor to Italy, no matter how long the visit may be, learning some Italian is never a bad idea. Italy was the cradle of Western civilization, from the Roman Empire to the Renaissance, and produced a unique cultural heritage. Italy is still the nexus of Western culture, be it in the arts, sciences, or food and wine. If a visitor learns Italian, they are bound to have a richer experience during their time in Italy, absorbing a robust background in humanities and art, by understanding Dante, Leonardo, Michelangelo and Brunelleschi, as well as coming to appreciate the genius of Armani, Ferragamo and Ferrari.

***Allora:*** A visitor's experience in Italy will be enriched and easier if the basic terms of polite greetings, directional questions, numbers, as well as shopping and food/restaurant Italian are learned before the vacation begins.

# How Italians See Themselves

**Heard in Trento:** "I wish we could set up our own country."

Visitors see Italians as largely homogeneous with, perhaps, some difference for those from Naples or Sicily. Among Italians, however, the different regions carry their own stereotypes within Italy. These reflect the thousand years of history in a largely isolated country that has been invaded by most everybody else.

Italians, in a linguistic version of "Name That Tune" can characterize a person having heard five words from his or her mouth. Those characterizations are blunt and strongly-held:

Abruzzi - The Abruzzo region is said to produce the most obstinate, skeptical, tradition-loving people in Italy.

Apulians - The Pugliesi, Apulians, are known to be proud, resilient and ironic opportunists.

Calabrians - People from Calabria are considered distrustful, violent and stubborn. They honor family above all else.

Friulians – People from Friuli, north of Venice are known for loving nature, being immobile, yearning for a return of the Austrian empire, and working hard.

Genoeses - People from Genoa are said to be *tirchi* or stingy, shy and unwelcoming.

Lucani - People from Basilicata are considered religious, individualistic, superstitious, and traditionalistic.

Marchigiani - People living in the Marche region value family above all else at home and in business. The philosophy of *localismo* is practiced throughout the region.

Milanese - People from Milan are renowned for being arrogant, cold, superior, efficient in the working world, entrepreneurial, and only interested in money.

Molisani - The region of Molise is said to produce the most reserved, sweet, family-loving people on the peninsula.

Neapolitans - People from Naples are considered cheerful, noisy, clever, superstitious and good at cooking pizza. They practice the art of "getting by."

Piedmontese - There is an Italian saying referring to people coming from Piedmont: *Piemontese falso e cortese*, which means people from Piedmont are false and kind. Also, they are found to be stingy, picky, and rigid.

Romagnole - People from Romagna are famous for being passionate, greedy and fighters. But they are also said to be cheerful, cordial, and tolerant.

Romans - Five adjectives are often attributed to people from Rome: noisy, skeptical, lazy, friendly and *burini*, boorish. Despite the the fact that the nation's capital is in Rome, the citizens are said to have no civic sense.

Sardinians - The islanders are said to be proud, melancholic, poetic, and lovers of the land.

Sicilians - People from Sicily are labeled as *omertosi*, meaning that they don't talk, especially when it comes to denouncing offenses. Sicilians are also famous for their jealousy, passion and generosity. They avoid anything having to do with governmental authority.

Trentini - The people of Trentino-AltoAdige are called the "Germans of Italy" because of their preference for the German language, tenaciousness, standoffish, and autonomous stands in opposition to federal control.

Tuscans - Tuscans are called *mangiafagioli* (bean eaters) and they're known for loving nature, being anti-religious, intolerant of stupidity and sarcastic. (Florentines are seen as snobbish, chronically unhappy, proud and unfriendly.)

Umbrians - Umbrians are associated with generosity, self-sufficiency, kindness and discretion.

Valdostani - From the northern region of Val d'Aosta, the Valdostani are known to be timid, mountaineers, and traditionalists.

Venetians - Venice produces people who are fatalistic, loyal, humorous, productive, and know how to party.

***Allora:*** Tourists to Italy tend to think that the Italians are the luckiest people on earth. They have the birthplace of the Renaissance, the best food in the world and a seemingly innate sense of style. What's not to love about being Italian and living by the Italian Life Rules?

# THE AUTHOR

Five years used to be Ann Reavis' attention span for any career. She's been a lawyer, a nurse, a presidential appointee in a federal agency, a tour guide and a freelance writer. She's lived in New Mexico, Texas, California (San Francisco Bay Area), Michigan and Washington, DC.

But in 1998, Ann fell in love with Italy and moved to Florence. She lived there, writing and working as a tour guide for sixteen years. She still shares her thoughts on Florence, Tuscany, and all things Italian in a travel and food blog – TuscanTraveler.com.

Italian Food & Life Rules is a compilation of earlier two books – *Italian Food Rules* (2013) and *Italian Life Rules* (2014).

# Original Copyrights

## ITALIAN FOOD RULES

Copyright © 2013 Ann J. Reavis
All rights reserved.

ISBN-13: 978-1512188646
ISBN-10: 1512188646

Published by Caldera Books
Email: calderabooks@gmail.com

Cover by Kelly Crimi
Interior book design by Bob Houston eBook Formatting

Without limiting the rights under copyright reserved above, no part of this publication may be reproduced, stored in, or introduced into a retrieval system, or transmitted, in any form, or by any means (electronic, mechanical, photocopying, recording, or otherwise) without the prior written permission of the copyright holder of the book.

Second Edition (June 1, 2015)

## ITALIAN LIFE RULES

Copyright © 2014 Ann J. Reavis
All rights reserved.

ISBN-13: 978-1512188776
ISBN-10: 1512188778

Published by Caldera Books
Email: calderabooks@gmail.com

Cover by Kelly Crimi
Interior book design by Bob Houston eBook Formatting

Without limiting the rights under copyright reserved above, no part of this publication may be reproduced, stored in, or introduced into a retrieval system, or transmitted, in any form, or by any means (electronic, mechanical, photocopying, recording, or otherwise) without the prior written permission of the copyright holder of the book.

Second Edition (June 1, 2015)

Made in the USA
Coppell, TX
18 June 2023

18253488R00218